Tracing your Family History using Irish Newspapers and other Printed Materials

FAMILY HISTORY FROM PEN & SWORD BOOKS

Birth, Marriage & Death Records
The Family History Web Directory
Tracing British Battalions on the Somme
Tracing Great War Ancestors
Tracing History Through Title Deeds
Tracing Secret Service Ancestors
Tracing the Rifle Volunteers
Tracing Your Air Force Ancestors
Tracing Your Ancestors
Tracing Your Ancestors from 1066 to 1837
Tracing Your Ancestors Through Death Records – Second Edition
Tracing Your Ancestors Through Family Photographs
Tracing Your Ancestors Through Letters and Personal Writings
Tracing Your Ancestors Using DNA
Tracing Your Ancestors Using the Census
Tracing your Ancestors Using the UK Timeline
Tracing Your Ancestors: Cambridgeshire, Essex, Norfolk and Suffolk
Tracing Your Aristocratic Ancestors
Tracing Your Army Ancestors
Tracing Your Army Ancestors – Third Edition
Tracing Your Birmingham Ancestors
Tracing Your Black Country Ancestors
Tracing Your Boer War Ancestors
Tracing Your British Indian Ancestors
Tracing Your Canal Ancestors
Tracing Your Channel Islands Ancestors
Tracing Your Church of England Ancestors
Tracing Your Criminal Ancestors
Tracing Your Docker Ancestors
Tracing Your East Anglian Ancestors
Tracing Your East End Ancestors
Tracing Your Family History on the Internet
Tracing Your Female Ancestors
Tracing Your First World War Ancestors
Tracing Your Freemason, Friendly Society and Trade Union Ancestors
Tracing Your Georgian Ancestors, 1714–1837
Tracing Your Glasgow Ancestors
Tracing Your Great War Ancestors: The Gallipoli Campaign
Tracing Your Great War Ancestors: The Somme
Tracing Your Great War Ancestors: Ypres
Tracing Your Huguenot Ancestors
Tracing Your Insolvent Ancestors
Tracing Your Irish Family History on the Internet
Tracing Your Jewish Ancestors
Tracing Your Jewish Ancestors – Second Edition
Tracing Your Labour Movement Ancestors
Tracing Your Legal Ancestors
Tracing Your Liverpool Ancestors
Tracing Your Liverpool Ancestors – Second Edition
Tracing Your London Ancestors
Tracing Your Medical Ancestors
Tracing Your Merchant Navy Ancestors
Tracing Your Northern Ancestors
Tracing Your Northern Irish Ancestors
Tracing Your Northern Irish Ancestors – Second Edition
Tracing Your Oxfordshire Ancestors
Tracing Your Pauper Ancestors
Tracing Your Police Ancestors
Tracing Your Potteries Ancestors
Tracing Your Pre-Victorian Ancestors
Tracing Your Prisoner of War Ancestors: The First World War
Tracing Your Railway Ancestors
Tracing Your Roman Catholic Ancestors
Tracing Your Royal Marine Ancestors
Tracing Your Rural Ancestors
Tracing Your Scottish Ancestors
Tracing Your Second World War Ancestors
Tracing Your Servant Ancestors
Tracing Your Service Women Ancestors
Tracing Your Shipbuilding Ancestors
Tracing Your Tank Ancestors
Tracing Your Textile Ancestors
Tracing Your Twentieth-Century Ancestors
Tracing Your Welsh Ancestors
Tracing Your West Country Ancestors
Tracing Your Yorkshire Ancestors
Writing Your Family History
Your Irish Ancestors

Tracing your Family History using Irish Newspapers and other Printed Materials

A Guide for Family Historians

NATALIE BODLE

Pen & Sword
FAMILY HISTORY

First published in Great Britain in 2024 by
PEN AND SWORD FAMILY HISTORY
An imprint of
Pen & Sword Books Ltd
Yorkshire – Philadelphia

Copyright © Natalie Bodle 2024

ISBN 978 1 39906 228 2

The right of Natalie Bodle to be identified as Author of this work has been asserted by her in accordance with the Copyright, Designs and Patents Act 1988.

A CIP catalogue record for this book is available from the British Library. All rights reserved. No part of this book may be reproduced or transmitted in any form or by any means, electronic or mechanical including photocopying, recording or by any information storage and retrieval system, without permission from the Publisher in writing.

The publisher has no responsibility for the persistence or accuracy of URLs for any external or third-party internet websites referred to in this book, and does not guarantee that any content on such websites is, or will remain, accurate or appropriate.

Typeset by Mac Style
Printed and bound in the UK by CPI Group (UK) Ltd,
Croydon, CR0 4YY.

Pen & Sword Books Limited incorporates the imprints of After the Battle, Atlas, Archaeology, Aviation, Discovery, Family History, Fiction, History, Maritime, Military, Military Classics, Politics, Select, Transport, True Crime, Air World, Frontline Publishing, Leo Cooper, Remember When, Seaforth Publishing, The Praetorian Press, Wharncliffe Local History, Wharncliffe Transport, Wharncliffe True Crime and White Owl.

For a complete list of Pen & Sword titles please contact
PEN & SWORD BOOKS LIMITED
47 Church Street, Barnsley, South Yorkshire, S70 2AS, England
E-mail: enquiries@pen-and-sword.co.uk
Website: www.pen-and-sword.co.uk
or
PEN AND SWORD BOOKS
1950 Lawrence Rd, Havertown, PA 19083, USA
E-mail: uspen-and-sword@casematepublishers.com
Website: www.penandswordbooks.com

Dedicated to my mum Jean with thanks for her unstinting love and support.

CONTENTS

Acknowledgements viii
Introduction ix
Abbreviations xii
Case Study One xiii
Case Study Two xix
Case Study Three xxiv
Case Study Four xxvii

Chapter 1   Newspapers in Libraries and Archives   1

Chapter 2   Online Newspaper Collections   11

Chapter 3   Transcriptions, Abstracts and Indices from Newspapers   19

Chapter 4   Periodicals and Journals   33

Chapter 5   Biographies and Genealogies   41

Chapter 6   The Gazette   49

Chapter 7   Almanacs and Street Directories   53

Chapter 8   Gazetteers and Topographical Dictionaries   69

Chapter 9   Online Libraries and Portals   80

Chapter 10   Book Publishers   91

Appendix: Useful Addresses 94
Bibliography and Sources 116
Index 117

ACKNOWLEDGEMENTS

I would like to thank a number of people and organisations who provided help in the compilation of this book.

Monica Cash, Samantha McCombe and Andrew at the Linen Hall Library provided guidance on their collections and additional background material.

Catherine Morrow of Libraries NI shared her knowledge and provided assistance at the Belfast Newspaper Library.

The British Library Board have kindly granted permission to use a number of images from newspapers through The British Newspaper Archive (**www.britishnewspaperarchive.co.uk**). All rights are reserved.

The National Library of Ireland, Ancestry, New England Historic Genealogical Society and the Local Government Management Agency (Ireland) also kindly provided permission to use images.

Finally, my thanks go to Internet Archive, Google Books, JSTOR, Hathi Trust and the Wellcome Collection for providing wonderful repositories of freely accessible books, journals and images.

INTRODUCTION

'Journalism is the first rough draft of history.'
Philip L. Graham

The information contained within newspapers is often seen in terms of global events such as wars, famine, revolution, natural disasters, space exploration, coups or the death of world leaders. In these cases, journalism is, as Philip Graham said, the first rough draft of history.

Crucially, journalism is not only about those large seismic global events that can impact on millions; it is also those small-scale events that are of interest to an insignificant number of people but that were reported upon in local newspapers around the country.

The British Newspaper Archive describes the main categories of items to be found in newspapers as follows:

- News articles – national events as well as issues of local and regional importance. These are your window into historical life.
- Family notices – birth, marriage and death notices plus related announcements including engagements, anniversaries, birthdays and congratulations.
- Letters to the editor written by the newspaper's readers, including illuminating contemporary debates, aspirations and anxieties.
- Obituaries – a wealth of contemporary information on the lives of notable individuals and ancestors.
- Advertisements – these include classifieds, shipping notices and appointments, illustrations such as photographs, engravings, graphics, maps and editorial cartoons.

Growing up in the market town of Ballymena situated in the middle of County Antrim, newspapers were part of the fabric of life. Dad bought one of the London-based national papers every day and a copy of the local, weekly *Ballymena Guardian* was always purchased. It was always flicked through to see if anyone we knew was mentioned in an article or was included in a photograph.

For years, my mum had on display a photograph of very toothy 9-year-old me with terrible hair, holding up a cup I had won for scripture at Sunday School. The story and photograph had been published in the local newspaper and I remember the local journalist coming to our house to take the photograph. It must have been very slow news week! This story wasn't of any interest to anyone other than our immediate family, but it was an event that was captured in a local newspaper and it adds to the story of an individual and their family.

My elderly uncle, on the other hand, bought the *Belfast Newsletter* every day mainly to examine the death notices to see if there was a wake or a funeral he felt that he should attend.

His brother and a friend took the 7-mile bus journey from their countryside home into Ballymena each Saturday evening in order to get a copy of *Ireland's Saturday Night* (also known as *The Pink*). They read the sports news and a few hours later got the bus home again – such was the height of their entertainment in rural County Antrim in the 1950s.

The earliest newspaper published in Ireland is believed to be *An Account of the Chief Occurrences of Ireland* which was printed in Dublin in February 1660 but ran for only a few issues. In the first half of the eighteenth century, 165 newspapers were launched in Dublin alone. Taxes were imposed on Irish newsprint in 1774 and this was not repealed until 1855. The resultant drop in prices combined with rising literacy rates led to a dramatic increase in the number of titles; by 1879, 127 titles were published outside Dublin.

Newspapers often reflected sectarian and political divides with many of the nineteenth-century publications owned by local and national politicians. When researching a story, it is often worthwhile seeking it out in different publications to ascertain if a different slant has been given.

Today though, we hear of titles going out of production on a regular basis, casualties of social media and the availability of twenty-four hours a day TV news channels and websites.

Thankfully, we have archives of newspapers – maybe part of your ancestor's story is waiting to be found within them?

This book deals with Irish newspapers, journals and periodicals that may be found in physical libraries and online repositories, but there is much more to found here.

The book includes information on biographies and genealogies; how to find your ancestor in the official record, *The Gazette*; how to track them down in street directories. It covers a range of online libraries, portals and book publishers who have a focus on Irish genealogy material. Throughout the book, there are hints and tips, case studies and excerpts that show you the type of material you can find on your ancestors, their lives and where they lived. Finally, there is a comprehensive list of addresses of key libraries, museums and archives where you can find further information by searching their online resources or catalogues.

ABBREVIATIONS

BNA	British Newspaper Archive
ACPL	Allen County Public Library
CIGO	Council of Irish Genealogical Organisations
DIB	Dictionary of Irish Biography
DNB	Dictionary of National Biography
DRI	Digital Repository of Ireland
FULS	Federation of Ulster Local Studies
GROI	General Register Office of Ireland
GRONI	General Register Office of Northern Ireland
GSI	Genealogical Society of Ireland
IGRS	Irish Genealogical Research Society
IFHS	Irish Family History Society
IHO	Irish History Online
IMC	Irish Manuscripts Commission
NAI	National Archives of Ireland
NEHGS	New England Historic Genealogical Society
NIFHS	North of Ireland Family History Society
NLI	National Library of Ireland
PHSI	Presbyterian Historical Society of Ireland
PRONI	Public Records Office Northern Ireland
RIA	Royal Irish Academy
SOG	Society of Genealogists
UHF	Ulster Historical Foundation

CASE STUDY ONE

The Murder of Hugh William Bradshaw on 24 April 1869

The death registration of Hugh William Bradshaw recorded that he was a married 40-year-old gentleman who died on 24 April 1869 at Philipstown. The cause of death was given as gunshot wounds by some person or persons unknown and death was immediate. The information had been provided to the registrar at Grean, Tipperary, Counties Limerick and Tipperary, by Tobias Morissey, the Coroner for County Tipperary on 14 May 1869.

This sad death of a relatively young man certainly required further research as the death registration seemed to suggest murder rather than death by Hugh Bradshaw's own hand. The newspapers were bound to have more information and they did not disappoint.

> **THE MURDER OF MR. BRADSHAW—THE INQUEST.**
>
> PHILIPSTOWN HOUSE, MONDAY.—This day, at half-past twelve o'clock, Dr. Morrissy, Coroner, held an inquest in the open air, outside the residence of the deceased lamented gentleman, the interior of the house being too small to accomodate the large concourse of persons that had assembled, and the day was beautifully fine. Amongst the magistrates present were:—Colonel E. B. Purefoy, D.L.; Henry Murray, U. Bayley, Samuel Cooper, Hefferman Considine, John Massy, Vere Hunt, Newport White, J. Bokin, R.M.; Captain Hemsworth, County Inspector; Sub-Inspectors Mullarky and Alderworth; Messrs William and John Bradshaw, brothers of deceased; his brother-in-law, Mr. Conway, and several other relatives.
>
> The jury then proceeded to view the body, and upon their return the following evidence was taken:—

The Sligo Champion, 1 May 1869. (British Newspaper Library)

The *Sligo Champion* published on 1 May 1869 reported on the inquest held following the death of Hugh William Bradshaw at Philipstown, County Tipperary.

The report provides interesting background information about Philipstown House, the home of the deceased where the inquest was held. It was too small to accommodate everyone who had gathered. From this report, we have the names of Dr Morrissy, the coroner, along with the names of the magistrates, the county inspector and the sub-inspectors.

The brothers of the deceased were named as William and John Bradshaw, while his brother-in-law was Mr Conway. The report refers to Mrs Bradshaw, the wife of the deceased, although her name is not provided. Two of the witnesses appeared to disagree as to whether the couple were on good terms with each other.

The witnesses who were examined included:

- Richard Mockler, Mr Bradshaw's coachman
- Constable Ross Parks of Cappawhite (the nearby village)
- John Coleman, 'a deaf and dumb man, able to read and write well'
- Mrs Smart, a domestic servant
- Dr John Ryan and Dr Robert A. Webb who carried out the post-mortem
- Margaret Ryan a domestic servant

We learned from the witness testimony that Mr Bradshaw had good relations with his tenants, but that he had received a threatening letter around December 1867.

The inquest found that death had occurred due to gunshot wounds and recorded an open verdict: 'That Hugh William Bradshaw was wilfully murdered on his own lands at Philipstown, County Tipperary, on the morning of the 24th of April 1869 by some person or persons unknown.'

The farmers of the neighbourhood offered a large reward for the discovery of the murderer.

A tantalising comment was provided by the Dublin correspondent of *The Times* who wrote, 'An impression now prevails that the murder of Mr Bradshaw was not agrarian, but originated in feelings of jealousy, excited by the habits of the deceased.'

(From the 1760s, agrarian violence was a feature of rural Ireland – secret societies and agricultural labourers instigated acts of violence and even murder against tenant farmers and landlords in protest at their management of their land and estates.)

If the murder was not linked to Bradshaw's management of his lands, what could the habits that created feelings of jealousy possibly be? Who was jealous? What further information could be gleaned from the papers?

A Dublin newspaper, *The Nation*, also carried the story in its 1 May 1869 edition, providing the additional information that Mr Bradshaw was a Justice of the Peace for Tipperary, that he was 'a harmless and inoffensive man and stood well with his tenants and workpeople' and that Philipstown House was near Cappawhite. That report gave a much more gruesome account of the injuries sustained by Mr Bradshaw (eleven wounds to the head) and also reported that the son of a tenant had been arrested for the murder.

A search of the Will Calendars held on the National Archives of Ireland website provides further intriguing information.

The will of Hugh William Bradshaw, late of Phillipstown House, County Tipperary Esquire, deceased, who died 24 April 1869 was proved at the Principal Registry (Dublin).

The will calendar reads as follows:

> The will of Hugh William Bardshaw late of Phillipstown House, County Tipperary, Esquire, deceased, who died 24 April 1869 at same place was proved at the Principal Registry by the oaths of Thomas Bolton Pennefather of Thurles, County Tipperary, Attorney-at-Law and Alicia Weldon of Highfort, Liscarroll, County Cork (wife of Robert Weldon, the Executors. (By Decree Pennedfather v. Hurley, 26 October 1869).

The interesting snippet is the last sentence which reads 'By Decree Pennefather v. Hurley, 26 October 1869.'

This suggests that there was a dispute about Hugh Bradshaw's will and a search of the newspapers using the term 'Pennefather v. Hurley' provided reports of the case that was heard in the Court of Probate before Judge Warren and the County Special Jury.

The *Irish Examiner* published on 28 October 1869 devoted a considerable amount of column space to the hearing. In essence, the defendant, Mr Hurley, who was the brother-in-law of Hugh William Bradshaw, contested the will on the grounds that Bradshaw had been of unsound mind and under the influence of the plaintiff, Mr Pennefather, and others. Hurley based his conclusion on the grounds that he believed Hugh Bradshaw was a man of intemperate habits who drank alcohol and took laudanum. Presumably, this was what *The Times* correspondent was referring to when he mentioned the habits of the deceased.

An acquaintance, Mr Vere Dawson Short, gave evidence to the effect that he had met Bradshaw earlier in 1869. Short said Bradshaw looked ill and had said he was disturbed in mind about his affairs. He advised Bradshaw to set his affairs in order and to consult Mr Pennefather.

Short also testified that Bradshaw had complained about his relationship with his wife, who he claimed had hit him with a saucepan, and that he was considering divorcing her.

Bradshaw's will of 1865 had made his wife's relations the beneficiaries, but he changed it in 1869 making his sister, Alicia Weldon, and her three sons the beneficiaries.

Alicia gave evidence stating that her brother had been beaten by his wife, who he had referred to as a devil.

Mr Pennefather's testimony confirmed that there were bad relations between Bradshaw and his wife. Furthermore, Pennefather said that he was acting upon the instructions of Mr Bradshaw and denied that he had ever influenced him in any way.

Mr Pennefather named some of the bequests, including £60 a year to Mr Bradshaw's illegitimate child and £350 to himself.

Various witnesses were interviewed and asked whether they were aware of Mr Bradshaw being a 'tippler', although this allegation seemed to be unsubstantiated.

The judge noted that Mr Hurley had been unable to produce witnesses to justify his claims that Mr Bradshaw had been under undue influence and found for the plaintiff, awarding him costs.

The information contained in these newspaper reports provide so much rich information and a back story that simply could not be gleaned from the official records such as the will calendar or Hugh Bradshaw's death certificate. From the available information, we can start to build a family tree as we have the names of Hugh's brothers and his sister Alicia, along with her married name of Weldon.

We know that Hugh's brother-in-law was a Mr Hurley; a search of the civil marriage records shows that Hugh William Bradshaw, the son of Hugh Brady Bradshaw married Maria Theresa Hurley, daughter of John Hurley on 11 January 1858 at Tralee Church of Ireland, County Kerry. Hugh William was described as an Esquire, as were his father and John Hurley, while Maria was described as a Lady.

We know that Hugh had an illegitimate child but we do not have her name or her date of birth; was she born before or after Hugh's marriage

1	a	**PHILIPSTON.** (Ord. S. 51.) Hugh Brady Bradshaw, Esq.		Rev. William Guinness,	House, offices, and land	133	3	28	117	10	0	16	15	0	134	5	0
–	b	Denis Ryan,		Hugh B. Bradshaw, Esq.	Gate house,	–			–			0	10	0	0	10	0
–	c	James Higgins,		Hugh B. Bradshaw, Esq.	House and garden,	0	1	5	0	1	0	0	9	0	0	10	0
		John Croagh,	⎱		Land,				0	1	0	–			0	1	0
		Michael English,			Land,				0	1	0	–			0	1	0
		Terence Kelly,			Land,				0	1	0	–			0	1	0
2		Thady Tracy,		Rev. Wm. Guinness,	Land,	10	1	18	0	1	0	–			0	1	0
		Edmund Ryan,	⎰		Land,				0	1	0	–			0	1	0
		James Tracy,			Land,				0	1	0	–			0	1	0
		Mary Mockler,			Land,				0	1	0	–			0	1	0
		Thady Ryan,			Land,				0	1	0	–			0	1	0
–	a	Thomas Cummins,		Edmund Ryan,	House and garden,	0	0	30	0	2	0	0	8	0	0	10	0
3		Thady Tracy,		Rev. William Guinness,	House and land,	10	0	37	10	0	0	1	0	0	11	0	0
4	a	Michael English,		Rev. William Guinness,	House, offices, and land	40	0	6	37	5	0	3	5	0	40	10	0

Griffith's Valuation – Philipstown, Parish of Donohill, Tipperary South Riding. (National Library of Ireland)

to Maria Hurley? Might the birth of this child be the cause of the jealousy referred to by *The Times* Dublin correspondent?

We also have a picture of the lifestyle of the couple – a gentleman farmer who had good relations with his tenants, who lived a comfortable life with servants and served his community as a Justice of the Peace. This is borne out by the information contained in the land valuation records.

Griffith's Valuation for Tipperary South Riding and the parish of Donohill is dated 1850. At that time, Hugh Brady Bradshaw Esq. was leasing from Rev. William Guinness, 133 acres, 3 roods and 28 perches of land valued at £117 10s and a house with an annual value of £16 15s in the townland of Philipstown. This substantial property leased by Hugh's father is likely to be the same property later occupied by Hugh Bradshaw and his wife Maria Theresa.

The newspapers in this case have provided a picture of unhappy family relationships and a man who lost his life too young.

Sources

Deaths (CR) Ireland. Grean, Tipperary, Counties Limerick and Tipperary. 24 April 1869. Bradshaw, Hugh William. Entry No: 52. GRO Ireland.

Sligo Champion. 1869. 'The Murder of Mr Bradshaw – The Inquest'. 1 May. Page: 3. Col: 7. Irish Newspapers at British Newspaper Archive. **www.britishnewspaperarchive.co.uk**

The Nation. 1869. 'Murder in Tipperary'. 1 May. Vol: XXVI. No: 37. Page: 8. Cols: 1–4. Irish Newspaper Archive.**www.irishnewsarchive.com**

Testamentary Records. Ireland. Principal Registry, Dublin. Date of death: 24 April 1869. Date of probate: 26 October 1869. Bradshaw, Hugh William. Will Calendar. Collection: Calendars of Wills and Administrations, 1858–1922. **www.willcalendars.nationalarchives.ie**

Irish Examiner. 1869. 'Mr Bradshaw's Will. Court of Probate. Tuesday. (Before Judge Warrend and County Special Jury)'. Pennefather v. Hurley. 28 October. Page: 3. Cols: 4–5. Irish Newspaper Archive. **www.irishnewsarchive.com**

Marriages (CR) Ireland. Tralee, County Kerry. 11 January 1838. Bradshaw, Hugh William and Hurley, Maria Theresa. Entry No: 85. **www.civilrecords.irishgenealogy.ie**

Valuation Rolls. Ireland. Philipstown, Parish of Donohill, Tipperary South Riding. 1850. Occupier: BRADSHAW, Hugh Brady. Lot: 1a. Page: 50. **www.griffiths.askaboutireland.ie**

CASE STUDY TWO

Joseph Gordon, Engineer, Publican, Confectioner and Restauranteur

On 9 September 1896, Joseph Gordon married Frances Annie Flatman. He was an engineer living in Belfast, the son of Alexander Gordon, also an engineer. His bride was the daughter of George Flatman, a tailor. The couple married in Cliftonville Presbyterian Church, Belfast, County Antrim.

Joseph Gordon had previously owned a licensed premises in Galgorm Street, Ballymena, which he sold at public auction on 22 December 1898. According to the advertisement for the sale in the *Ballymena Observer* of 16 December 1898, it was a thriving business and one of the oldest established spirit concerns in Ballymena. The premises came with a shop and dwelling house, stores and office, and a very large shed fitted up with loose boxes and stalls capable of accommodating 100 head of cattle and horses. Mr Gordon had established good connections with cattle dealers and had carried on this trade for the past three years.

His reason for selling was because he had bought 'at a high price' the licensed premises of the late Mr John P. Mewhirter in another part of Ballymena but the new premises were not suitable for the accommodation of cattle.

On 28 September 1900, an advertisement in the *Ballymena Observer* provided notice of a sale by public auction of a licensed premises in Mill Street, Ballymena owned by Mr Joseph Gordon. It comprised two shops and dwelling houses held by lease for a term of sixty years from 1 November 1882 at the yearly rent of £26. The premises were being sold because Mr Gordon had recently acquired the licensed premises of his brother in Cullybackey which required his entire time and attention.

The spirit licence was a seven-day retail licence and the premises were described in the notice as having been recently considerably extended and developed, with ample accommodation for a large number of people.

With a little expenditure it was claimed, it could be turned into a desirable hotel capable of accommodating fifty persons. A considerable sum had been spent on the premises and the house was fitted with a bath. There was a commodious yard in the rear with a separate entrance from Wellington Street and stabling for a large number of horses – on market and fair days, it was always fully occupied.

The other shop and premises were immediately adjoining the licensed premises and they were currently let to a tenant who paid £15 per annum.

The Belfast and Province of Ulster Directory 1889 shows that William Gordon, a publican and the likely brother of Joseph, was recorded as an inhabitant of the village of Cullybackey.

The 1901 Census of Ireland shows that Joseph was a 40-year-old Presbyterian spirit merchant who was living with his 30-year-old wife Francis [sic] Annie, a seamstress, 2-year-old daughter Cathrine [sic], 1-year-old son Frederick and 4-month-old son Alexander. Twenty-year-old Maud Flatman was a visitor.

The family were living in the village of Cullybackey, near Ballymena, County Antrim. They were not living above a licensed premises but in

NOW OPEN.

JOSEPH GORDON

DESIRES TO INFORM his friends and the public generally that he has taken over those old-established premises occupied by

The late Mr. WILLIAM M·KEE,

Wholesale and Retail Confectioner, Pastry and Biscuit Manufacturer,

72 CHURCH STREET,

BALLYMENA,

Having secured the services of an experienced and Competent Baker, he is in a position to turn out up-to-date Crusty Loaves, Tea Rolls, Scones, etc., as well as High-Class Pastry, in the most careful, dainty, and satisfactory style.

BREAKFASTS, DINNERS, and TEAS supplied in a manner and at terms that defy competition. Every attention given to patrons.

SUITABLE STOCK OF ALL THE REQUIREMENTS OF THE TRADE.

B-615

Ballymena Weekly Telegraph, 5 September 1908. (Courtesy of British Newspaper Archive)

> **Tea Table Temptation.**
>
> One feels tempted to eat so much—that is the only drawback to
>
> **Our Cakes and Pastry.**
>
> Their superiority is due to the fact that we make a special and careful study of the art of Baking, and use only the very best ingredients. Breadcart makes daily rounds of Ballymena and District, and will call specially at any place on intimation being given. When you want anything tempting in the Pastry or Confectionery way, be sure and come to
>
> **GORDON'S,**
>
> **72 CHURCH STREET, BALLYMENA.**

Ballymena Weekly Telegraph, 30 October 1909. (Courtesy of British Newspaper Archive)

a dwelling house which had seven rooms and five windows in the front and was of second class. The property had six outhouses: a stable, a coach house, a harness room, a barn, a store and a forge.

In 1908, Joseph Gordon opened a bakery and restaurant in premises at 72 Church Street, Ballymena, County Antrim that had formerly been occupied by William McKee as shown in this advertisement in the *Ballymena Weekly Telegraph* published on 5 September 1908.

In 1909, Joseph was placing notices in the local press advertising his cakes and pastry and also their breadcart that made daily rounds of Ballymena and district, such as this one in the *Ballymena Weekly Telegraph* of 30 October 1909.

In 1910, Joseph Gordon was listed in the *Belfast and Ulster Towns Directory* as a Wholesale and Retail Confectioner, Restaurant and Bakery.

However, on 23 September 1910, Joseph M. Gordon of Church Street, Ballymena was adjudged bankrupt – a small entry in the *Irish News and Belfast Morning News* published on 1 October 1910 noted that the judgement has been published in the *Dublin Gazette* the previous evening.

On 12 December 1910 the *Belfast Newsletter* carried an advertisement for the former bakery premises:

> Splendid Opening – To Let, large shop and commodious dwelling-house, 72 Church Street, Ballymena: old established confectionery

and pastry bakery: tea rooms attached, where highly successful business was long conducted by the late William McKee.

The two years that Joseph had been running the business were ignored – was it due to a concern that a short-lived business was not viable and might not attract investors?

On 3 March 1911, the *Ballymena Observer* carried an advertisement for the sale of the contents of 72 Church Street and it seems that household goods as well as shop fittings were up for sale.

The 1911 Census of Ireland, taken just a month after this advertisement, shows that 51-year-old Joseph M. Gordon, a Presbyterian millwright was living at house 6 Woodvale Road, Belfast. At the same property were his 43-year-old wife Francis A., a shopkeeper who was Methodist and had been born in India, his 13-year-old daughter Kathleen Betrice, 10-year-old son Alexander Francis, 6-year-old son Ernest B. and 2-year-old son William R.

The property was a shop with five rooms and three windows in the front, and the house was of second class. No outhouses were recorded.

As may be seen from the information gleaned from the newspapers, there is a much richer back story to be found for the Gordon family than is available in the census records or in the couple's marriage record.

The articles build a picture of the lives of the Gordon family – Joseph seems to have moved from one business to another quite rapidly and seemed to like variety in his work. Even after his bankruptcy, he wasn't put off being in the retail trade, although it was his wife who was the named shopkeeper rather than Joseph.

Ballymena Observer, 3 March 1911.
(Courtesy of British Newspaper Archive)

MESSRS. LANCASTER & CO.'S SALES.

Important Sale by Auction.

AT 72, CHURCH ST., BALLYMENA, this day and following days, at 3 and 7 o'clock.

MESSRS. LANCASTER & CO

Will sell by Auction, the whole of the valuable stock of China, Cutlery, Jewellery, etc., comprising — MARBLE CLOCKS, Bronze Figures, Regulator Clocks, Gold Rings, Gold Watches, China Clock Sets, SILVER TEA AND COFFEE SETS, Art Vases, Plant Pots, Cases of Fish Eaters, Carvers, Table and Dessert Knives, Spoons. Forks, Leather Bags, Purses, etc.

Sale each day at 3 and 7 o'clock.   01.

It appears that the property at 72 Church Street, Ballymena lay vacant until it was taken over by Miss Annie Cousley in 1916. The Valuation Revision Books do not note any other occupants between Joseph Gordon and Annie Cousley and no records of advertisements or entries in street directories were found that suggest new tenants.

Sources

Marriages. Ireland. Cliftonville, Belfast, County Antrim. 9 September 1896. Gordon, Joseph and Flatman, Frances Annie. Entry No: 23. **https://civilrecords.irishgenealogy.ie**

Ballymena Observer. 1898. 'Mr Petticrew's Sales. Valuable Spirit Licence in Ballymena for sale by auction'. 16 December. Page: 8. Col: 4. Collection: Irish newspapers at British Newspaper Archive .

Street Directory. Ireland. Cullybackey, County Antrim. 1899. Gordon, William. *The Belfast and Province of Ulster Directory 1899*. p.1316. Collection: Street Directories online at PRONI. **https://streetdirectories.proni.gov.uk**

Ballymena Observer. 1900. 'Mr Petticrew's Sale Valuable Leasehold Premises for sale by public auction in Mill Street, Ballymena'. 28 September 1900. Page: 4. Col: 2. Collection: Irish newspapers at British Newspaper Archive.

Census. Ireland. Cullybackey, Galgorm DED, Poor Law Union, Ballymena, County Antrim. House 4. 31 March 1901. Gordon, Joseph. Forms A, B1 and B2. www.census.nationalarchives.ie

Ballymena Weekly Telegraph. 1908. 'Now Open', Joseph Gordon. 5 September 1908. Page: 1. Col: 3. Collection: Irish newspapers at British Newspaper Archive.

Ballymena Weekly Telegraph. 1909. 'Tea Table Temptation'. 30 October. Page: 1. Col: 4. Collection: Irish newspapers at British Newspaper Archive.

Street Directory. Ireland. Church Street, Ballymena, County Antrim. 1910. Gordon, William. *The Belfast and Ulster Towns Directory*. (Transcript). Collection: Street Directories online at Library Ireland. **www.libraryireland.com/UlsterDirectory1910/Ballymena-9.php**

Irish News and Belfast Morning News. Ireland. 1910. 'Bankruptcy'. 1 October. Page: 2. Col: 7. Collection: Irish newspapers at British Newspaper Archive.

Belfast Newsletter. Ireland. 1910. 'Country and Seaside Houses'. 12 December. Page: 2. Col :1. Collection Irish newspapers at British Newspaper Archive.

Ballymena Observer. Ireland. 1911. 'Messrs Lancaster & Co's Sales'. 3 March. Page: 12. Col: 6. Collection: Irish newspapers at British Newspaper Archive.

Census. Ireland. Woodvale Road, Belfast, Woodvale DED, County Antrim. House 6. 2 April 1911. Gordon, Joseph. Forms A, B1 and B2. www.census.nationalarchives.ie

CASE STUDY THREE

The Marriage of James and Winifred Grealish on 10 February 1909

On 10 February 1909, the marriage took place of James Grealish, a 28-year-old bachelor and farmer who lived at Carnmore, the son of Peter Grealish, a farmer.

The bride was Winfred Grealish, a 20-year-old spinster with no occupation, the daughter of James Grealish, also a farmer.

The marriage was conducted at Castlegar Roman Catholic chapel in the registrar's district of Galway, County Galway.

So far, so good, and there is nothing in this record to hint at any drama or concern.

Belfast Newsletter, 16 February 1909. (Courtesy of British Newspaper Archive)

WEDDING PARTY GUARDED BY POLICE.
Extraordinary Scene at Castlebar.

An extraordinary scene has been witnessed at a Roman Catholic wedding in Castlebar. A young man named Grealish, son of a farmer who is boycotted, and whose house was attacked by armed men a day or two ago, was married under protection of the police, who guarded the chapel throughout the ceremony.

After the wedding there came the "dragging home," a local custom. The bride and bridegroom on a side car were at the head of a procession of about forty cars, in which rode the guests who had been invited to the wedding. The rere of the cavalcade was brought up by the police mounted on bicycles.

On arrival at Carnmore, the future home of the bride, it was found that a large force of constables, armed with rifles, had been sent there by the authorities, who feared that after the attack on Mr. Grealish's house there might be a renewal of hostilities. Everything, however, passed off quietly.

LIFE IN IRELAND.

A Diary of Outrages, etc., under Radical Rule.

"I am not going to palliate or minimise the deplorable state of things which exists in some parts of Ireland. I and my colleagues would be false to our duty and false to our real opinions if we did anything of the kind. I quite admit that there are going on in some parts of Ireland things which are reprehensible, which ought to be put down, which public opinion ought to condemn, and which, so far as the arm of the law is strong enough to reach them, the arm of the law ought never to be slack in reaching and preventing."—Mr. Asquith, House of Commons, February 16.

Statement by Mr Asquith as reported in the Index to Irish Facts, Vol 3, 1910. (Courtesy of Internet Archive)

However, a search of the newspapers produced an intriguing report in the *Belfast Newsletter* of 16 February 1909 of an armed police guard at the wedding and the information that Peter Grealish, the groom's father, had been boycotted.

It should be noted that the newspaper report provides the place name as Castlebar which is in County Mayo, but the actual place is Castlegar in County Galway as recorded on the marriage registration.

Although no further reports in relation to Peter Grealish were found within BNA newspapers, a Google search using the term 'Peter Grealish boycotted 1909 Galway' gave results for a book entitled *Index to Irish Facts*, Vol 3, published by the Union Defence League – this is freely available at Internet Archive.

The statement by Mr Asquith, British Prime Minister between 1908 and 1916, refers to the unrest in Ireland at the time.

Events involving the Grealish family that were reported in the newspapers were provided in the book, as follows:

> On 10 February in County Galway – The house of a man named Peter Greelish [sic] of Oranmore, was fired into between 7 and 8 o'clock at night, but no person was injured. The police were communicated with, and they arrested a man in whose house a recently discharged gun and several rounds of ammunition were found. It is alleged that the prisoner threatened Peter Greelish and his son on a former occasion.
>
> Extract from Index to Irish Facts – Report carried in the *Dublin Daily Express*, 11 February 1909.

A report by the Galway correspondent of *The Irish Times* was published on 13 February 1909, similar to that in the *Belfast Newsletter* of 16 February 1909 (see image).

> On 26 February in County Galway – At a special court in Galway two men, named John Beatty and George Glynn, were charged with firing into the house of Peter Greelish, of Oranmore. They were both returned for trial, bail being allowed.
>
> Extract from Index to Irish Facts – Report was carried in the *Galway Observer*, 27 February 1909.

Note that the place name of Oranmore as reported in the book is in error as it should read Carnmore as noted on the couple's marriage registration.

Sources
Marriages. Ireland. Castlegar, Galway, County Galway. 10 February 1909. Grealish, James and Grealish, Winifred. Entry No: 50. **https://civilrecords.irishgenealogy.ie**

Belfast Newsletter. Ireland. 1909. 'Wedding party guarded by police'. 16 February. Page: 7. Col: 6. Collection: Irish newspapers at British Newspaper Archive.

Union Defence League. (1910) *Index to Irish Facts*. Vol 3. pp.112–13, 118, 175–76. London: Vacher and Sons Ltd. **www.archive.org**

CASE STUDY FOUR

The Great Famine

Following the 1798 United Irishmen Rebellion, the Act of Union of 1800 meant that Ireland lost its own parliament and was governed by England.

By 1820, Ireland had become one of the most densely populated countries in Europe with a population of about 6.5 million people with thousands unable to support themselves and their dependants.

There was high unemployment and the rents for many were too high to be affordable. Many labourers and small farmers relied on growing sufficient potatoes to feed their families and to have a small surplus to sell. Poverty was widespread and it was estimated that over 2 million people were at near starvation level in Ireland.

Various committees and commissions had reported on the state of the country and the living conditions, but little was done to address the issues. In one account to the House of Lords Select Committee on the State of Ireland in 1825, Daniel O'Connell described how the lower classes lived in one-room cabins built of mud that let in the rain, with whole families sleeping together. Their bedding was of straw and they had little, if any furniture. Their diet consisted of potatoes and buttermilk or water.

The Act for the Relief of the Destitute Poor in Ireland (The Poor Relief (Ireland) Act) was enacted in 1838.

The country was divided into Poor Law Unions that generally centred on market towns, and a workhouse was to be provided in each of the designated 163 Unions. Relief was only to be given to those who entered the workhouse and people were to be assisted to emigrate.

The potato had been introduced to Ireland in the mid-1700s. It was a crop that could grow in almost any soil, took little labour and its

One of the first reports of the potato blight on 11 September 1845 in the Freeman's Journal. (Courtesy of British Newspaper Archive)

DISEASE IN THE POTATO.

We refer to another part of our impression for details concerning this fearful visitation. We regret to have to state that we have had communications from more than one well-informed correspondent announcing the fact of the appearance of what is called "cholera" in potatoes in Ireland, especially in the north. In one instance the party had been digging potatoes—the finest he had ever seen—from a particular field, and a particular ridge of that field, up to Monday last. On digging in the same ridge on Tuesday, he found the tubers all blasted, and unfit for the use of man or beast. We are most anxious to receive information as to the state of the potato crop in all parts, for the purpose either of allaying unnecessary alarm, or giving timely warning. All through Fingal serious damage has been already sustained.

nutritious value contributed to the rise in the Irish population to over 8 million by 1841.

Other crops such as wheat, barley and oats were grown, but they were mostly exported, leaving the peasantry reliant on the potato to feed themselves and their families.

The potato crop had failed many times in the past due to weather conditions or disease and it was recognised as being an unreliable food source. One of the first reports of the blight was on 16 August 1845, when

The scene at the gate of the workhouse from Ridpath's History of the World, Vol 7. (Courtesy of Internet Archive)

The Gardeners' Chronicle and Horticultural Gazette reported 'a blight of unusual character' on the Isle of Wight.

On 11 September 1845, one of the first reports of a potato disease in Ireland was reported in the *Freeman's Journal*.

The blight, which was a fungal disease, could destroy a crop in the matter of a few hours, turning the plants into a mush.

The following year, it was clear that the crop had failed in most parts of the country and between 1845 and 1849, the potato crop failed in three seasons out of four. The result was starvation and the spread of dysentery, typhus and cholera.

Many were evicted from their homes because they could no longer pay their rent, and eventually thousands of people sought refuge in the workhouses. These did not have the capacity to cope with the numbers and so many were turned away – and subsequently died. Images such as the 'Scene at the gate of the workhouse' appeared in the press and alerted people throughout Britain and indeed the world to the grave situation in Ireland.

Eventually, a system of outdoor relief and a system of outdoor works in exchange for subsistence was introduced, although it was deemed inadequate. The millions of people lost to famine, disease and emigration meant that it took some areas of Ireland decades to recover and it is an event retained in the folk memory of the country.

Sources

Freeman's Journal. Ireland. 1845. 'Disease in the potato'. 11 September. Page: 2. Col: 5. Collection: Irish newspapers at British Newspaper Archive.

Ridpath, John Clark, (1907) *Ridpath's History of the World*. Vol 7. p.309. Cincinnati, Ohio: The Jones Brothers Publishing Company. p.309. **www.archive.org**

Chapter 1

NEWSPAPERS IN LIBRARIES AND ARCHIVES

There is such a wealth of information to be found in newspapers, from news of national importance to the mundane, local events of interest to only a few.

Although many publications have been digitised, indexed and made available online, there are still many more that are only available to view during an in-person visit to the library or archive where they are held.

This chapter covers the main repositories within the island of Ireland where you may view Irish titles – these collections are to be found in hardcopy and microfilm formats.

The Appendix provides a list of local libraries, archives and museums where you will find collections of printed material.

You may wish to undertake a research visit yourself or to hire a local researcher who can do the work on your behalf.

The Newsplan Project

If you are interested in researching an ancestor through newspapers, it will be helpful to know which titles were in existence at the time period in question and to have an idea whether news about them is more likely to be found in a national newspaper such as the *Irish News* or a local newspaper such as the *Coleraine Chronicle*.

Sadly, the recent redesign of the NLI website has seen the removal of the very useful Newspaper Database which allowed for searches of newspaper titles based on where they were published and included titles held in the NLI and other locations.

However, the information is now available on the NLI catalogue as a digitised book. *The Report of the Newsplan Project in Ireland*, 1998,

London and Dublin may be found at **https://catalogue.nli.ie/Record/vtls000042992**

The NLI describes the Newsplan project as one that originated in the mid-1980s as a co-operative preservation project for newspapers in Ireland and the United Kingdom. Northern Ireland and the Republic of Ireland make up one of the ten regions through Ireland and the UK.

The aim of the project was to preserve newspapers while allowing access and it was agreed that microfilm produced to archival standard was the best means of doing this. Each region produced a report listing its holdings of existing files of newspapers and allocated priorities for microfilming. The original 1992 report was revised twice and is now available as an online book.

The report provides an alphabetical list of Irish newspaper titles, the town and dates of publication, and where copies may be found.

You will notice that there are non-Irish places such as Boston, Montreal, Melbourne, New York, Toronto, Sydney and even Buenos Aires listed in the report. For example, the San Francisco edition of the *Irishman* began publication there in 1979 and the NLI holds a hardcopy for September 1979.

The Leader was published in San Francisco between 1934 and 1939 and the NLI holds hard copies from 20 January 1934 to 26 August 1939.

Generally, the Irish-based newspapers are going to be of more help when tracing your ancestors who were resident in Ireland. If your ancestors hailed from, for example, County Fermanagh, browse to find titles published in that county.

One of the earliest titles for County Fermanagh is the *Enniskillen Chronicle and Erne Packet*. The entry records that the *Chronicle* was published between 10 August 1808 and 31 May 1849. It then continued as the *Fermanagh Mail and Enniskillen Chronicle* between 23 August 1849 and 27 July 1893, then merged with *The Impartial Reporter*. The NLI holds the following copies:

Microfilm:
- 1824–31 May 1849

Hardcopy:
- 26 November 1808
- 28 April 1810
- 3 October 1811
- 1885–1892

You can also search the catalogue for a specific newspaper title and further information will be provided about the NLI's holdings.

Note that the catalogue does not give online access to the titles listed. The NLI does not have online newspapers, but you can visit in person.

The oldest newspaper held in its collection is *An Account of Chief Occurrences in Ireland* published in February 1660, although it only ran for a few issues.

National Library of Ireland, Dublin

The Dublin Society (which later became the Royal Dublin Society after a Royal Charter was granted) was established in 1731. Mainly concerned with improvement in matters of agriculture, manufacture and art, the government acknowledged its usefulness with an annual grant. In 1836, a recommendation was made to consider the Society's library as a National Library; access to the general public was improved and acquisitions became more general with an emphasis on Irish material.

The National Library and Museum was established in 1877 and is now based at Kildare Street, Dublin.

Note when visiting NLI that hardcopy newspapers will not be issued if the publication is available in microfilm.

National Library of Ireland. (Credit Yvonne M, Wikimedia Commons)

If you plan to visit the NLI in person, you need a Reader's Ticket which can be applied for in advance. Further information about Reader's Tickets may be found at **www.nli.ie/visit/readers-ticket**

NLI provides a copying service – see **www.nli.ie/collections/using-our-collections/copying-services** for more information.

Newspaper Library, Belfast

The Newspaper Library in Belfast has the largest collection of newspapers available to the public in Northern Ireland.

The collection dates from the eighteenth century and includes almost complete runs of the Belfast newspaper titles. Of particular note is the *Belfast Newsletter* from 1759 along with rare and unique holdings of the *Northern Star* and the *Londonderry Journal* 1796–1801.

Its collection includes Irish political and radical newspapers, as well as periodicals such as the *Irish Catholic* and *Farm Weekly*.

Newspapers from across the island of Ireland are to be found here, including a complete run of *The Irish Times* and the *Irish Independent* along with national newspapers published in England such as *The Times*, *The Guardian* and *The Financial Times*.

The library buys newspapers each day and, on a six-monthly basis, sends them off to be bound. Recent editions are available in the adjoining Belfast Central Library while the bound and microfilm versions are found in the Newspaper Library.

Many of the library's holdings are in large bound volumes such as the earliest surviving editions of the *Northern Star*, the newspaper of the Society of United Irishmen. It was published from 1792 to 1797 and featured articles by leading members of the society with a mixture of

The 1794 hardcopy volume of the Northern Star in the Newspaper Library, Belfast. (Courtesy Natalie Bodle)

political comment, international and local news. The Newspaper Library has copies from 1793.

A list of titles held on microfilm by Libraries NI is available at **http://bit.ly/3OOl6zz**

Note that on this list, the Newspaper Library is referred to as the Heritage Library and that the list does not include the titles held in hardcopy. Contact the Newspaper Library to find out what titles and dates it holds.

Libraries Ireland

A list of the libraries within Libraries Ireland may be found at **www.librariesireland.ie**. You can find further information about the catalogue and access to online books, magazine and newspapers here too.

Each of the main county libraries that tend to hold the genealogy and local history collections are listed in the Appendix.

Libraries NI

A list of Libraries NI locations may be found at **www.librariesni.org.uk/Libraries/**. Within this list are nine libraries with cultural heritage collections containing a range of materials of interest to the family historian, including newspapers held on microfilm and hardcopy. The list of libraries with cultural heritage collections may be found at **http://bit.ly/3OZhqef**.

Each of the heritage libraries has its own information sheet with a summary of their notable collections. The cultural heritage libraries are:

- Ballymena Central Library, County Antrim
- Belfast Central Library and the Newspaper Library, County Antrim
- The Newspaper Library is covered above. Of note in Belfast Central Library are cuttings files – articles on personalities, places and events that have been selected from local papers for over 100 years. It also has current files of over seventy-five daily, weekly and Sunday newspapers covering the whole of Ireland.
- Derry Central Library, County Londonderry
- Downpatrick Library, County Down
- Enniskillen Library, County Fermanagh. The collection includes historic newspapers from 1825 up to the present day. Holdings for the two current Fermanagh newspapers are *The Impartial Reporter* 1825–2010 and *The Fermanagh Herald* 1902–2017.
- Mellon Centre for Migration Studies, County Tyrone. Of note is the *Londonderry Journal* on microfilm 1772–1887 (incomplete) and the *Tyrone Constitution* 1845–1855.

- Newry City Library, County Down
- Omagh Library, County Tyrone. Of note is the Omagh Bomb Archive. On the afternoon of Saturday, 15 August 1998 at approximately 3:10 p.m., a car bomb exploded in Market Street, Omagh, killing 29 people and two unborn children, as well as injuring some 370 people. It remains the largest loss of life of any single incident in the history of the Northern Ireland Troubles. The archive includes more than 13,000 newspaper articles, more than 30,000 emails, 840 books of condolence and 53 videos with news clips from UTV, the BBC and RTE.
- Cultural Heritage Service Library Armagh, County Armagh

A useful addition to the services of Libraries NI is the Civic Access Borrower Scheme. If you are current member of Libraries NI and aged 18 or over, you can apply to join the Ulster University Library as a borrower. For more information see **www.ulster.ac.uk/library/services/borrowing-and-access-schemes/civic-access-borrower-scheme**

Linen Hall Library, Belfast

Founded in 1788, the Linen Hall is the oldest library in Belfast and the last subscribing library in Ireland. It is renowned for its Irish and Local Studies Collection, ranging from comprehensive holdings of early

The earliest surviving copy of the Belfast Newsletter from October 1738. (Courtesy of The Linen Hall Library)

Belfast and Ulster printed books to the 250,000 items in the Northern Ireland Political Collection, the definitive archive of the recent Troubles.

The newspaper collection dates from 1738 with unparalleled holdings of the *Belfast Newsletter* and a complete run of the *Northern Star*, the newspaper of the Society of United Irishmen, among the highlights.

It has an excellent genealogy department with records that include the Joy Manuscripts, the Blackwood Pedigrees, a range of school registers, a good selection of street directories, individual family histories and a wide array of genealogy reference books.

The catalogue and further information about the collections may be found at **www.linenhall.com**.

The Linen Hall Library Postcard Collection contains more than 7,000 images which capture Ireland in bygone days and gives a sense of

The entrance to the Linen Hall Library, Belfast. (Courtesy of the Linen Hall Library)

what life was like in remote villages and towns over 100 years ago. The Postcard Collection may be found at **www.postcardsireland.com**.

Dublin City Library and Archives

Dublin City Library and Archives contains records of the civic government of Dublin from 1171 to the late twentieth century. These records include city council and committee minutes, account books, correspondence, reports, court records, charity petitions, title deeds, maps, plans and drawings, all of which document the development of Dublin over eight centuries.

National and local newspapers, some dating from the eighteenth century, are also held in the library. Newspapers continue to be collected on an ongoing basis and are available to the public in digital or microfilm formats. Some newspapers are available in hardcopy.

An alphabetical list of titles held by Dublin City Library and Archives is to be found here: **http://bit.ly/3VF2e8c**.

Dublin City Library subscribes online to *The Irish Times* Newspaper Archive and the Irish Newspaper Archives, which give access to a searchable electronic archive of newspaper titles.

It may be necessary to book an appointment and to pre-order items. Contact details are included in the Useful Addresses in the Appendix.

Daily newspapers are available for reading in Dublin Libraries' Business Information Centre in the Central Library, Ilac Centre, Henry Street, Dublin 1.

Marsh's Library, Dublin

Marsh's Library in Dublin was built by Archbishop Narcissus Marsh (1638–1713) and it was the first public library in Ireland. It was designed by Sir William Robinson (died 1712) the Surveyor General of Ireland, and is one of the very few eighteenth-century buildings left in Dublin still being used for its original purpose. The library opened in 1707.

The interior of the library, with its beautiful dark oak bookcases each with carved and lettered gables, topped by a mitre, and the three elegant, wired alcoves or cages where the readers were locked in with rare books, remains unchanged since it was built over 300 years ago. It is a magnificent example of an eighteenth-century scholars' library.

Today, it is open to visitors – booking is advised and an admission fee is payable. Guided tours are also available.

Marsh's Library has a collection of newspapers that may be viewed in person. The collection of Dublin newspapers is the largest, and titles held by the library may be found in its catalogue, which provides extensive descriptions: **www.marshlibrary.ie/catalogue/**.

The catalogue shows, for example, that *Saunder's News-Letter and Daily Advertiser* was published in Dublin by J. and E. Potts in 1803. Marsh's Library holds 131 issues between 1 January and 31 December 1803 with two leaves in each edition. They are generally of good to very good quality with a small number stained or excessively cropped. They are bound in modern cloth with a collection of newspapers and form part of the Benjamin Iveagh Collection.

Public Records Office Northern Ireland (PRONI), Belfast

PRONI is the official archive of Northern Ireland and it has a selection of newspapers on microfilm that may be viewed on site. The collection includes titles from Belfast, Dublin and some provincial towns.

Most of the microfilms contain runs of a specific newspaper with a Northern Ireland or Ulster focus, such as the *Newry Examiner* issues between 1830 and 1837, the *Ulster Bulletin* issues between 1922 and 1925 or the Dublin based *Freeman's Journal* issues between 1763 and 1800.

There is also a microfilm (PRONI Reference: MIC/457) with miscellaneous Irish newspapers published in Dublin that contains copies of very early (late seventeenth-century to early eighteenth-century) copies of the *Dublin Intelligence*, the *Flying Post* and the *Dublin Post*.

In addition to the publications on microfilm, there are hardcopy newspapers to be found in other collections. These tend not be full runs, but are sometimes just a few newspapers, or cuttings on various subjects that have been mixed in with other documents such as family papers, etc. For example, PRONI Reference D1229/1 contains only one copy of

PRONI, Belfast in the shadow of Harland and Wolff's famous cranes. (Courtesy Discover NI)

the *Drogheda Journal* dated 20 April 1914 and one copy of the *South Down Herald and County Down Independent* dated 24 April 1902.

The list of newspapers held at PRONI are to be found at **www.nidirect.gov.uk/publications/newspapers-available-microfilm**.

PRONI'S e-catalogue may be searched for more detailed information about the contents of each microfilm or reference. There is useful browse facility for the e-catalogue which may be found at **http://bit.ly/3I8xBVd**.

If you are visiting PRONI in person, you need to have a PRONI visitor pass; more information about obtaining a pass may be found at **https://bit.ly/3VMRuVj**.

Chapter 2

ONLINE NEWSPAPER COLLECTIONS

Of course, it is not always going to be possible to visit archives or libraries in person and undertaking visits in person is a time-consuming process. It is of great benefit to genealogists across the world that a growing number of newspapers have been digitised, indexed and made available online, allowing for searches for your ancestor and the place where they lived, along with all manner of local and world events.

Choosing a Subscription

It is worthwhile checking which publications are available before paying for a subscription. A search for publications available for my home county of Antrim on the Irish Newspaper Archive shows twenty-three publications listed with a range of years. On closer inspection, however, these newspapers are either national (all Ireland) or regional (Northern Ireland) and there are none specifically for my hometown of Ballymena.

Having checked the Newsplan Project at NLI (see Chapter One) there are thirteen titles that were published in Ballymena, the earliest of which was the *Ballymena Observer* from 1855.

The British Newspaper Archive has thirty-six publications for County Antrim, most of which are national or regional. However, there are four Ballymena publications and it may the case that my ancestors were not named in the regional papers but only in the local titles.

Irish Newspaper Archive

Describing itself as 'the world's largest and oldest online database of Irish newspapers' the Irish Newspaper Archive has over 6 million pages of content from across Ireland, dating from 1738 to the present day.

It is possible to filter according to newspaper, by date, by county of publication and of course to search for keywords. Searching is free but you must subscribe to see the article you are interested in.

A number of the newspapers available on Irish Newspaper Archive such as *Sunday World*, *The Drogheda Independent*, the *Derry Journal*, the *Longford Leader* and *The Ulster Herald* have editions up to the present day.

In addition to traditional titles, this site provides access to a range of radical newspapers, many of which had short runs. These publications are mostly concerned with workers' rights or with nationalist or republican ideals – some of the titles included within the Radical Newspaper Archives are:

- *The Belfast Strike Bulletin* – three editions were published in 1919.
- *The Bottom Dog* – Limerick's first working-class paper. This weekly publication was written and circulated by some of the leaders of the Trades Council and continued for forty-eight editions to 1 November 1918.
- *Prison Bars* – the Organ of the Womens' Prisoners Defence League. Edited by Maud Gonne McBride, this was a feminist journal that published objections to the Irish Constitution from prominent female nationalists (regarding the status of women in Article 41.2 as a betrayal of the 1916 promise of 'Equal Rights and Equal Opportunities for all citizens'). Published on the first of each month there were twenty-one editions between 1937 and 1938.
- *The Irish War News* – only one edition was ever published which was during the 1916 Easter Rising and it was edited by Patrick Pearse. *The Irish War News* was created to spread the word of the rebellion and its front page carried the news that the Irish Republic had been declared in Dublin.
- *The Dalcassian* – only one edition was ever published in 1919 in Ennis, County Clare to show support for shophands who had gone out on strike in 1919.
- *The Irish Worker's Voice* – the official newspaper of the Communist Party of Ireland and was published weekly on and off between 1931 and 1936, running to 264 editions.
- *The Spark* – an anti-British publication. There were sixty-four editions published in Dublin between 1915 and 1916.

The full list of available titles in both archives and further information about subscriptions may be seen at **www.irishnewsarchive.com/ subscribe**.

Subscriptions are available on a monthly or annual basis and with access to either only the Radical Newspaper Archive or the Newspaper Archive, or for both archives.

The British Newspaper Archive (BNA)
The British Library's collection of historical newspapers contains newspapers from 1603 to the present day, from Britain, Ireland and further afield. There are over 600,000 bound volumes of newspapers and over 300,000 reels of microfilm. In the past, the only way to view this collection was to visit the British Library in London in person.

In 2011, the BNA was launched – a partnership between the British Library and Findmypast to digitise and make millions of pages of fully searchable newspapers available online. There is a very good collection of national and provincial Irish titles with more being added all the time. The titles that have been digitised are listed at **www.britishnewspaperarchive.co.uk/home/NewspaperTitles**.

The BNA website **www.britishnewspaperarchive.co.uk** allows you to search for free but you must pay to see the results. There is a useful browse facility that allows for filtering based on date, country, region, county, place and recently added titles.

The Advanced Search option is very good as it allows for searches based on keywords, exact phrase, the exclusion of certain words along with the type of article such as Advertisement, Article, Family Note, Illustrated, Miscellaneous, Table or Front Page Article.

BNA has four subscription options:

- Monthly
- Three monthly
- Twelve months
- Pay as you go

However, be aware that with certain subscriptions for Findmypast, you also have access to all of the digitised newspapers on BNA. Be sure to check and don't pay for access twice.

Findmypast Subscription
www.findmypast.co.uk

If you subscribe to Findmypast and have either a Pro or Premium account, you also have access to the BNA's British and Irish newspapers.

Although it is possible to filter according to British or Irish titles, by date, place, county, newspaper or article type, the search function on the

Where to find the Newspapers and Periodicals Collection at Findmypast.

newspaper part of Findmypast's site is not as powerful as that found on BNA's website.

One option to reduce the number of search results you may get on Findmypast is to carry out your search on BNA and then filter on Findmypast's site to access the articles you are interested in.

Free Access to Newspapers on BNA and Findmypast

Both BNA and Findmypast provide free access to over 400 titles which includes the following Irish titles:

- *Drogheda News Letter*, 1813
- *Waterford Chronicle*, 1827–1871
- *Sligo Observer*, 1828–1831
- *Dublin Weekly Herald*, 1838–1842
- *Tralee Chronicle*, 1843–1880
- *Waterford News*, 1848–1869
- *United Irishman*, 1848
- *Cork Advertising Gazette*, 1855–1859
- *Meath People*, 1857–1863
- *Cavan Observer*, 1857–1864
- *Skibbereen and West Carbery Eagle; or, South-Western Advertiser*, 1861–1870
- *Munster Express*, 1869–1871
- *Leinster Independent*, 1871–1872
- *Dublin Shipping and Mercantile Gazette*, 1871

The Irish Times Archive
www.irishtimes.com/archive
The Irish Times is published in Dublin and distributed throughout Ireland every Monday to Saturday. It was first published on 29 March 1859 and today it provides a print version along with an online version that allows a certain amount of free access to current articles before it goes behind a paywall.

Digital subscribers can view reproductions of every page of *The Irish Times* from 1859 to the present day.

Subscribers can search by date and keyword. Subscriptions may be standard or premium and can be paid for on a monthly or an annual basis.

The more expensive premium subscription provides online access to *The Irish Times* exactly as it appears in print.

The Church of Ireland Gazette
The *Church of Ireland Gazette*, formerly known as the *Irish Ecclesiastical Gazette* has been digitised and made freely available online. The database covers the years 1856–2010 and it is possible to search by keywords or to browse the issues.

Published in Dublin, this paper carried advertisements for schoolteachers, clergy missionaries, letters, discussion on doctrine and general church news, etc.

Not all of those named were members of the Church of Ireland, as shown in the 19 December 1865 edition which carried a list of those who had passed the examinations for Dublin University, for entry into the Indian Civil Service, for Direct Commissions in the Army and for admission into the Royal Military Colleges of Woolwich and Sandhurst. Pupils of Kingstown School (a Church of Ireland school) were distinguished in the list by having their names printed in italics.

Later editions of the paper have photos of parishioners and clergy. The *Church of Ireland Gazette* may be found at **https://bit.ly/3k93wGR**.

Newspapers by Ancestry
This is a subscription website owned by Ancestry with billing every six months.

It describes itself as the largest online newspaper archive with over 819 million pages of historical newspapers from over 25,900 newspapers.

By far the greatest number of titles are from the United States, followed by Canada. There are titles from Panama, Australia, New Zealand, Ireland and the United Kingdom (which includes Northern Ireland).

The Irish and Northern Irish titles are of limited quantity, although if you have a subscription it is worthwhile carrying out a search for your Irish ancestors. It is likely, however, that you will have more success in either the Irish Newspaper Archive or BNA / Findmypast. In addition, those websites offer more flexible payment options.

The Newspapers by Ancestry archive may be found at **www.newspapers.com**.

Ancestry Card Catalogue

If you have a subscription to Ancestry, do not overlook its newspaper collections.

The records that you will be able to access will depend upon the type of subscription you pay for and your country of residence. Further information is available at **www.ancestry.com**.

Under the Search tab, select the Card Catalogue and then Newspapers and Periodicals.

Escape from Kilkenny Gaol. Leinster Journal, 11 August 1802. (www.ancestry.co.uk)

You can filter by location – options include United Kingdom, Northern Ireland and Ireland. It is worthwhile filtering separately for each of these because of the way the record sets have been classified. For example, the *Irish Genealogical Abstracts from the Londonderry Journal 1772–1784* are within Northern Ireland and United Kingdom records but not in the Ireland records.

The Ireland, Newspapers, 1763–1890 record set contains thirty Irish newspapers printed between 1763 and 1890. These titles may be browsed but they are not indexed and are not searchable by name or place.

A report in the *Leinster Journal* of 11 August 1802 recorded that on 16 May 1802, three men, Terence Maher, Michael Butler and Richard Conway, broke out of Kilkenny Gaol. The report gave detailed information about where the men had been living, what offences they were found guilty of, what they were wearing when they escaped and a physical description of each man.

This is genealogical gold-dust as it provides information that very few of us have for our ancestors who lived over 200 years ago. This information would not have been found when searching under Ancestry's record search because the names have not been indexed.

Other record sets of interest on Ancestry within Newspapers and Periodicals that have been indexed and are searchable by name are:

- Ireland, *Police Gazettes*, 1861–1893
- Belfast, Northern Ireland, the *Belfast Newsletter* (Birth, Marriage and Death Notices), 1738–1925
- Irish Genealogical Abstracts from the *Londonderry Journal* 1772–1784
- UK and Ireland, Obituary Index, 2004–Current
- *Irish Independent* Newspaper Obituaries, May 2001–June 2002
- The Public Register or *Freeman's Journal* (Dublin, Ireland)

An example of a very informative article in the Irish Genealogical Abstracts from the *Londonderry Journal* of 9 May 1777 is the following:

```
Londonderry.
Ads: Hugh Hill and William Lecky, executors of William Hogg, deceased, and
William Ross (William Lecky and William Ross being heirs of William Hogg) vs.
Isaac Read, Mary Read otherwise M'Manus his wife, George Hart, only son of
Eliz. Hart otherwise M'Manus, deceased, and Meredyth Workman, only son of
Jane Workman otherwise M'Manus, deceased (Mary Read, George Hart, and
Meredyth Workman being heirs of Charles M'Manus, deceased); D. Ross,
deceased, late executor of William Hogg; lands lately held by Charles M'Manus
to be sold; rent roll is with Aeneas Murray, plaintiff's attorney.
```

Londonderry Journal, 9 May 1777. From Irish Genealogical Abstracts from the Londonderry Journal, 1772–1784. (www.ancestry.co.uk)

This is particularly valuable because it explains a number of family relationships; it is all the more useful because it covers a time almost 100 years prior to the civil registration of births and deaths in Ireland – when records proving family relationships can be difficult to find.

Google News

Google News has a selection of newspapers, most of which are from the United States and Canada. There are a few English and Scottish titles but few, if any, Irish published papers.

However, if your ancestor emigrated, you may find a record within these free-to-view pages. Do be aware that for some titles there are only a few editions and coverage can be patchy. Some titles published abroad with an Irish focus and available on Google News are:

- *The Irish Sentinel* – published in Quebec, Canada
- *The Irish Vindicator and Canada General Advertiser* – published in Montreal, Canada
- *The Irish Canadian* – published in Toronto, Canada

The Google News site is searchable and of course, many of the newspapers published abroad carried news of events in Ireland and Northern Ireland.

Although this would not be my first-place go-to site for Irish-based research, it is still worth carrying out a search on your ancestor's name or place of residence to see what it brings up. It may be more useful for any family members who emigrated to the United States or Canada.

The site may be found at **www.news.google.com/newspapers**.

Joseph McGarrity Newspaper Collection

Villanova University in Pennsylvania has a number of freely available online collections, one of which is the Joseph McGarrity newspaper collection, which includes newspapers, periodicals and serials. A number of these were published in Ireland or have an Irish focus. It is possible to search within the collection, which is to be found at **https://digital.library.villanova.edu**.

Chapter 3

TRANSCRIPTIONS, ABSTRACTS AND INDICES FROM NEWSPAPERS

In Ireland, the civil registration of non-Roman Catholic marriages commenced in 1845 and Roman Catholic marriages commenced in 1864, while civil registration of birth and deaths commenced in 1864.

Birth, marriage and death announcements in newspapers, therefore, can provide very useful biographical information to help to build a family tree, identify previously unknown family members, confirm family relationships, and reveal home addresses and burial locations. They can also help to identify the church that a family belonged to, thereby giving vital information about which church records it might be useful to search for your ancestors.

Entries can provide some unexpected information such as this marriage announcement in *Pue's Occurrences* of 4 July 1758: 'Mr. Thomas Neile of Shinrone in the King's County [now County Offaly], aged 18 [was married] to Mrs. Elizabeth Naillor of Rutland in said County.' She was aged 80 and Thomas was her tenth husband!

Marriage announcement from Pue's Occurrences dated 4 July 1758. (British Newspaper Archive)

One wonders what on earth happened to the previous nine husbands and if Thomas managed to outlive his elderly wife.

A number of indices and transcripts of birth, marriage and death announcements along with obituaries have been compiled and made available – these have been detailed under the subheadings below.

In some cases, these have been provided in book format, others are in databases as part of a paid subscription, while others are freely available online databases or when visiting a library or archive.

It should be noted that poorer families didn't tend to place birth, marriage and death notices in newspapers as there was a cost to insert them. As a result, it is unlikely that you will find poor ancestors in these notices prior to the twentieth century.

Libraries Ireland and Libraries NI

It is always worthwhile checking with local libraries and particularly those that hold genealogy collections such as the county libraries in the Republic of Ireland and the Heritage Libraries in Northern Ireland.

An example of a local collection is that held by Clare County Library which has a collection of birth, marriage and death notices spanning the years 1824–1855, 1852–1854 and 1850–1855 respectively and were published in *The Clare Journal, Limerick Chronicle, The Times, The Clare Freeman, Dublin Evening Mail* and the *Freeman's Journal*.

The collection was created by Theobald Fitz-Walter Butler, Lord Dunboyne (1806–1881) and has been transcribed by volunteers and indexed by County Clare Library staff. It is part of the Lord Dunboyne Collection and is freely available online at **http://bit.ly/3HI1tHt**.

Indexes of marriages and deaths from *Pue's Occurrences* and the *Dublin Gazette*, 1730–1740

This index is held at the NLI, Ms. 3197. It was compiled by George Burtchaell and is not digitised nor currently available online.

Index for the *Belfast Newsletter*, 1737–1800

The *Belfast Newsletter's* first edition was in 1737 and it was published three times per week during the eighteenth century in issues of four pages each that covered both local and international news.

Every significant word and date in the 20,000 surviving pages of the newspaper was indexed, although not all of the newspapers are still available. In fact, only about one-quarter of the newspapers for the years from 1737 to 1750 have survived, although the run of newspapers is nearly complete from 1750 to 1800.

The surviving issues of the *Belfast Newsletter* between 1737 and 1800 are as follows:

- 1737 – Newspaper established *circa* 1 September. No extant issue.
- 1738 – First surviving issue is 3 October 1738. A few other issues survive.
- 1739–1745 – no surviving issues.
- 1746 and 1747 – a few surviving issues.
- 1748 – no surviving issues.
- 1749 – a few surviving issues.
- 1750 – nearly complete.
- 1751 – no surviving issues.
- 1752 – nearly complete.
- 1753 – very few surviving issues.
- 1754–1800 – virtually complete.

The final database of information contains nearly 300,000 items of news and advertisements.

The database was compiled by a team of indexers led by Dr John C. Greene under the aegis of the Institute of Irish Studies at the Queen's University of Belfast. It was prepared by and is hosted by the University of Louisiana at Lafayette, United States and is freely accessible. The option to complete a wildcard search is very useful, given the variety of spelling of Irish names and place names that exist. The database may be found here: **www.ucs.louisiana.edu/bnl**.

Note that the newspapers themselves are not available at this site, but if you find a reference of interest, you will be able to track down a copy of the edition of interest in an archive or online repository.

Index to Births, Marriages and Deaths in the *Belfast Newsletter*, 1738–1863

The Linen Hall Library in Belfast, Northern Ireland has two indexes to Births, Marriages and Deaths in the *Belfast Newsletter*:

- A bound volume index from 1738 to 1800
- A comprehensive alphabetical card index of Births, Marriages and Deaths in the *Belfast Newsletter* from 1801 to 1863

These indexes are available to search in person in the Linen Hall Library. Once a reference of interest has been found, the *Newsletter* newspaper itself may be consulted on microfilm in the library.

The Births, Marriages, Deaths Index to Belfast Newsletter 1738–1800 at the Linen Hall Library. (Courtesy of Natalie Bodle)

The Alphabetical Card Index of Births, Marriages and Deaths in the Belfast Newsletter at the Linen Hall Library. (Courtesy of Natalie Bodle)

Irish Genealogical Abstracts from the *Londonderry Journal*, 1772–1784

This book by Donald M. Schlegel was published by Baltimore in 1990 with a reprint in 2001. He abstracted all notices of marriages, births, deaths, separations, estate settlements, and persons emigrating to North America which appeared in the *Londonderry Journal* between 1772 and 1784.

There are 2,000 names within the book which has been indexed and is available to view on Ancestry with a subscription.

Alternatively, an inexpensive e-book may be purchased from Google Books: **https://books.google.co.uk**.

North of Ireland Family History Society Publications and Resources

Family History Societies often have a wealth of local information and dedicated bands of volunteers who spend time transcribing and indexing records that are helpful to others.

The North of Ireland Family History Society (NIFHS), as the name suggests, has a number of family history branches in the north of Ireland and a well-stocked research centre at Newtownabbey, County Antrim.

The NIFHS website at **www.nifhs.org** lists each of the branches with its contact details. The online shop stocks the following books of transcriptions of births, marriages and deaths from newspapers:

- Hatches, Matches & Dispatches – Omagh, County Tyrone. Almost 2,000 entries recorded from older newspapers that include the *Tyrone Constitution, Omagh News, Strabane Morning Post, Belfast Newsletter* and *Derry Journal*
- *The Ballymoney Northern Herald & Ulster General Advertiser*, Births, Marriages and Deaths. This 80-page book contains entries from 1860–1863
- The *Coleraine Chronicle*, Births, Marriages and Deaths 1844–1869 and *The Londonderry Sentinel*, Births, Marriages and Deaths 1829–1869. This was originally two separate publications but they have both been made available on a USB stick, which is available for purchase from the Causeway Coast and Glens branch of the NIFHS at **https://colerainefhs.org.uk**.

In addition to publications for sale, the NIFHS has within the Research Centre a range of Newspaper Indices. These may be consulted in person in the Research Centre or members of the society may request a look-up from volunteers.

The library list includes indices dating from 1737 from a variety of mainly northern titles. The library list may be found at **www.nifhs.org/resources/library-list/**.

The NIFHS also has on permanent loan, the genealogical correspondence of the Presbyterian Historical Society of Ireland (PHSI). This includes an Index of USA Obituaries mainly from the Bangor and Portland, Maine areas. The index may be viewed online at **http://bit.ly/3Gohxxo**.

An Irish wake, from a sketch by M. Woolf, 1873. (Library of Congress)

Another resource is Notes from Canada, which includes obituaries taken from newspapers. This may be viewed online at **http://bit.ly/3PYqj8u**.

Both of these resources are freely available to non-members.

The Genealogical Society of Ireland

The Genealogical Society of Ireland is based in Dún Laoghaire, Co. Dublin where it has a *An Daonchartlann* (archive). Its website is at **www.familyhistory.ie**.

Some years ago, the society obtained a collection of obituaries of Irish people who had died mainly in Canada with some in the USA and New Zealand. The collection consisted mainly of newspaper cuttings and also a few transcriptions of obituaries and gravestones. In most cases, the cuttings did not include the name of the newspaper or date of publication. However, the list of names does include the date and place of death, an age and a birthplace. This is quite specific in some cases, with the name of a town or townland; others provide just the county or Ireland. For some, the birthplace is not recorded at all.

These Obituaries of the Irish Diaspora records are free to view and may be found at **http://bit.ly/3jx1KmR**.

The Ulster Historical Foundation (UHF) Databases

The UHF is based in Newtownards, County Down where it has a research facility.

Members of the society can access a range of online databases at **www.ancestryireland.com/search-irish-genealogy-databases**. The databases that have records extracted from newspapers are as follows:

- Petition from the inhabitants of Bangor, County Down relating to the Act of Union, 31 January 1800. The Act of Union was passed in 1800 and came into force on 1 January 1801; thereafter the Irish parliament was abolished and Irish MPs represented their constituents at Westminster, London. Petitions for and against the Act of Union were drawn up, several of which were published in the *Belfast Newsletter* in 1799–1800. This list has the names of over 200 inhabitants from Bangor, County Down and was published in the *Newsletter* on 31 January 1800.
- *Northern Standard*, Birth, Marriage, Death notices, 1839–1847
- *Armagh Guardian*, Births, Marriages and Deaths, 1844–1852
- *Tyrone Constitution*, Deaths, 1882–1889
- Birth, Death and Marriage entries from the *Strabane Journal*, 1785–1787
- Petition of the Roman Catholic Inhabitants of Lower Creggan, County Armagh. This petition regarding the Act of Union contains the name of 460 individuals and was published in the *Belfast Newsletter* on 17 January 1800.
- Act of Union Petitions, 1799–1800. This petition regarding the Act of Union was signed by 888 individuals from counties Armagh and Down and was published in the *Belfast Newsletter*.
- Dublin Exchange, April 1815. On 24 April 1815, the Dublin Exchange building collapsed causing several deaths and numerous casualties. This list provides details of twenty people who suffered minor and more serious injuries. Occupations and other details are provided in a number of cases. The details were extracted from the *Strabane Morning Post* of 2 May 1815.
- Application to Register as Voters in the Barony of Armagh. This list of freeholders for the Barony of Armagh provides the name, residence and occupation of residents along with a description of the property and its annual value. Details extracted from the *Newry Commercial Telegraph* published on 3 October 1839.
- Applications to Register as Voters in the Barony of Tiranny. This list of freeholders for the Barony of Tiranny (County Armagh) provides the name, residence and occupation of residents along with a description of the property and its annual value. Details extracted from the *Newry Commercial Telegraph* published on 3 October 1839.

- Names regarding tenant-right in County Monaghan from *Freeman's Journal*
- Names of clergy and freeholders who were requesting a general meeting of the clergy, freeholders and landholders of the county at Castleblaney on Wednesday, 16 June to take effective measures to secure the triumph of tenant-right, in the return of Dr John Gray, the tenant-right candidate for the county, at the next general elections. Dated 1852.

The Irish Genealogical Research Society (IGRS)

The IGRS is a learned society established in 1936 with the aim of collecting copies of materials compiled before the 1922 Great Fire at the Public Record Office in Dublin. While it is based in England, it also has an Irish branch and worldwide membership.

The society describes its library and archive as one that is recognised worldwide as the most important collection of material on Irish genealogy held in private hands.

A number of databases are freely available online to non-members, while other material may only be accessed by members of the society.

The society has an extensive library where materials may be accessed in person. For some time, the IGRS library was co-located with the Society of Genealogists (SOG). In 2021, the SOG sold its building and moved out and the IGRS put its own library into storage. The intention is that in future, the IGRS library will be co-located in the new location of the SOG.

Early Birth, Marriage and Death Index

These indices provide information beyond parish registers and civil registration records. Non-members may search and will be given information on the number of entries for a particular name. The full transcript is available to members and it may be found at **www.irishancestors.ie/unique-resources**.

One example found in the Early Births Index is for a male child called Arthur Harper who was the son of John Harper, a gentleman. The record was dated 1800 in County Laois, Ireland. The source of the record was the Registry of Deeds, reference number 387841.

Captain Clanchy Marriage Index

Captain Henry Clanchy (1894–1966) was one of the IGRS's earliest members. During the 1950s he prepared an extensive card index of marriages gleaned from some of the society's unique manuscript collection and pedigree files.

Given the nature of the material he was consulting, the marriages tend to be those of the fairly well-heeled and well-connected, hence a high proportion of captains and majors, reverends, sirs, JPs and doctors are among the names recorded.

Geographically, the index covers the entire island of Ireland and there are nearly 6,000 entries.

These transcripts are freely available to download for non-members and may be found at **www.irishancestors.ie/unique-resources**.

An example of one of the transcripts for Helen Fagan, the daughter of Richard Fagan and Elinor Aylmer who married John Taylor *circa* 1670 and had one daughter.

Dr P. Smythe-Wood's Irish Newspaper Index. Series A – selected families mainly from County Tyrone
The late Dr Patrick Smythe-Wood presented a large collection of card indexes to the IGRS Library that reflected his various interests: the Irish in Canada; Ulster families; various professions, etc. These include abstracts from a number of Irish newspapers, including the *Belfast Newsletter*. The index may be found at **http://bit.ly/3GBt9x1**.

Dr P. Smythe-Wood's Irish Newspaper Index. Series B – families mainly from Ulster.
This index may be found at **http://bit.ly/3jP4Gvr**.

Dr P. Smythe-Wood's Irish Newspaper Index. Irish Prison Officers and their families
This series included newspaper sources as well other sources that included Succession Lists, Burke's Landed Gentry, gravestone inscriptions and those listed in various directories. This index may be found at **http://bit.ly/3Z4z0Cd**.

Dr P. Smythe-Wood's Irish Newspaper Index. Customs and Excise Officers and their families. Also Inland Revenue officers
This index may be found at **http:// bit.ly/3jHjtYR**.

Dr P. Smythe-Wood's Irish Newspaper Index. German families with Irish connections
This index may be found at **http://bit.ly/3Z8z1VW**.

The Dr P. Smythe-Wood's Irish Newspaper Indices may be viewed by non-members.

Eddie's Extracts

Eddie's Extracts is a labour of love by Eddie Connolly. His website has transcriptions of births, marriages and deaths from various (mainly Ulster-based) newspapers that include the *Belfast Commercial Chronicle*, the *Downpatrick Recorder*, the *Banner of Ulster*, the *Ulster General Advertiser*, the *Northern Whig*, the *Belfast Weekly News*, the *Belfast Morning News* and the *Belfast Daily Mercury*.

Also on the site are news clippings that include court reports, inquests, and subscriptions lists along with book extracts, church records, records of deceased seamen and the names of over 25,000 Presbyterians who served during the Great War of 1914–1918, and more.

The article below is an extract from the *Belfast Newsletter* dated Tuesday, 6 January 1801:

> A Special Vestry was held in the parish church of Comber [County Down], on Tuesday last, when it was resolved, that they would support their own poor, and that the travelling poor within that parish should be badged. Monthly subscriptions were then entered into for the relief of distressed householders, and a Committee appointed to ascertain their number, and grant badges on those deserving. Lord Londonderry, with his usual goodness and humanity, subscribed very generously; and Sir James Blackwood (not knowing what was done) *unsolicited*, sent the next day a liberal donation. It is hoped this example will be of use to stimulate other parishes to adopt similar reformations, that idle vagrants may be excluded who have no claim upon the benevolence of society.

It is possible to search on the website or simply browse by date. This website is freely available and may be found at **www.eddiesextracts.com**.

Nick Reddan's Newspaper Extracts

Nick Reddan's website includes extracts from various Irish newspapers from 1720 to 1865 and these are sorted by family name. The site has been supplemented by extracts compiled by Simon de Montfort sourced from the counties of Longford, Leitrim, Westmeath and Roscommon.

The following marriage notice from the *Westmeath Journal* of 24 December 1823 provides interesting information about family relationships that stretch beyond the shores of Ireland as well as information about the residences of some of the bridal party:

At Silvermines Church, near Nenagh [County Tipperary], on the 16th inst. by the Rev Dean Holmes, Vicar of Kilmore, Edward Bourne, Esq, Gloucester Street to Catherine, youngest daughter of the late Wm Carrol, Esq and sister of General Sir William P. Carrol, KCB, Lieutenant-Governor and Commander of the Forces in the island of Malta. The bride was given away by her cousin, General Bourke. After the ceremony, the party set off for Tulla House, the seat of Sir William Carrol.

The information on this website is freely available and may be found at **http://bit.ly/3VGHwo7**.

Ireland Old News
This website contains extracts from a range of newspapers and they are organised by county of publication, year and month. It is also possible to carry out a search for all articles on the site.

On this site there is also an Irish Death Notice Index with 54,867 names of people who were born and/or died in Ireland or whose deaths were mentioned in Irish newspapers. This includes 25,056 indexed entries from the *Cork Examiner* of the nineteenth and twentieth centuries along with 1,947 entries from the New York-based *Irish-American*.

In most cases, the obituary is not supplied, but the reference provided shows the name of the publication and the date; that will allow for a search in archives or online repositories.

The information on this website is freely available and may be found at **www.irelandoldnews.com**.

Belfast Timeline Project
The Belfast Timeline Project has transcribed newspaper entries from 1837 to 1941 that recorded events in Belfast. There is free access to PDF files – one for each decade apart from the 1900s – at **www.belfasthistoryproject.com/belfasttimeline**.

There are plenty of names recorded and a search may be carried out on each file using Ctrl+F keys.

Boston Pilot: Irish Immigrant Advertisements (*Search for Missing Friends*), 1831–1920
The American Ancestors website is hosted by the New England Historic Genealogical Society (NEHGS) at **www.americanancestors.org**.

Beginning in 1831 and over the course of the next eighty-five years, the nationally distributed *Boston Pilot* newspaper printed some 45,000

'Missing Friends' advertisements placed by friends and relatives. No one knows how many of these families found each other as a result of the adverts, but these nineteenth-century notices continue to help families today find their ancestors.

These advertisements typically referred to the exact place of origin of the seeker and/or the sought. Many of the adverts also describe the process and route of immigration, and even the name of the passenger ship. Many refer to women, for whom determining exact origin is even more difficult, due to the lack of naturalisation records. So, the Missing Friends notices help fill a great gap in nineteenth-century records for a mobile, impoverished, immigrant population.

The extract shown below is taken from Volume 3 of the *Boston Pilot* (1854–1856), page 256 and refers to three sisters from County Mayo who had emigrated around the same time and who were last heard of in New York.

OF ELLEN, Cath and Mary RAINEY, of parish Killeaden, co Mayo, who left Ireland in '48 or '49, and when last heard from they were living in Lawrence street, N Y. Address their cousin Patrick McLoughlin, care of Stephen Burke, 65 Water st, Cincinnati, O.

The Boston Pilot Irish Immigrants Advertisements database. (NEHGS www.americanancestors.org)

This database is searchable by first and last names, time period, volume of newspaper and last place of residence. It is freely accessible – just register for a free guest account to view the images. The database may be found at **https://bit.ly/3wpyb7n**.

Findmypast

As discussed in Chapter Two, Findmypast **www.findmypast.co.uk** has linked up with the BNA to provide access to digital images of newspapers which include a comprehensive selection of Irish titles.

In addition to access to the BNA, Findmypast also has records that include transcriptions from Irish newspapers or that feature Irish-born people.

It is possible to filter by location and type of record. In this case, filter by Irish records, then directories and social history collection which has a sub-category of newspapers and magazines.

Some of the record sets in this collection are:

- Irish Newspaper Transcript Archive, Ffolliott Collection 1756–1850. Rosemary Ffolliott was a celebrated Irish genealogist who compiled

this comprehensive catalogue of biographical notices from Irish newspapers.
- Ireland Newspaper Birth Notices. This record set has 42,605 birth announcements placed in one of three Irish publications, i.e. the *Belfast Morning News*, the *Champion* or *Sligo News* and the *Cork Examiner*.
- Ireland Newspaper Marriage Notices. This index has 68,760 entries compiled from announcements in the same three Irish publications recorded above.
- Ireland Newspaper Death Notices. This record set has 66,681 entries from the same three publications noted above. These records include 'in memorium' notices published on anniversaries of the death.
- Farrar's Index to Irish Marriages 1771–1812 – Baptisms. Farrar's Index by Henry Farrar was published in two volumes in 1897 and was extracted from entries in *Walker's Hibernian Magazine*. The baptism index comprises 125 records.
- Farrar's Index to Irish Marriages 1771–1812 – Marriages. Over 12,000 marriages are listed in this index providing addresses, names and addresses of the parents (often only the bride's father) and the date and place of marriage. Also included is an index by Sir Arthur Vicars that compiled the births, deaths and marriages recorded in the magazine *Anthologia Hibernica* (1793–1974) giving a total of over 14,000 names.
- Farrar's Index to Irish Marriages 1771–1812 – Deaths. There are 531 records in this set that can provide information such as name, age, date of death, cause of death, marital status and occupation.
- Quakers Annual Monitor 1849. Otherwise known as the Obituary of the Members of the Society of Friends in Great Britain and Ireland for the year 1848, this is a published list of obituaries and death notices compiled from the annual return of the Society's Meeting Houses in 1848 and the latter part of 1847.
- Irish Marriage Notices in American Newspapers. This record set includes 2,500 wedding notices that occurred in various countries and were recorded in the following American newspapers:
  - *The Brooklyn Eagle* (1841–1955)
  - *New York Herald* (1835–1924)
  - *New York World* (1860–1831)
  - *Phoenix* (1859–1861)
- Irish Death Notices in American Newspapers. This collection includes announcements of Irish people who died in America although some died in other countries such as Ireland or England. There are about 36,000 notices listed from the following publications:
  - *Chicago Citizen* (1882–1897)
  - *Chicago Tribune* (1847–present)

- *Illinois State Journal* (1848–1947)
- *New Orleans, Picayune* (1837–present)
- *New York Herald* (1835–1924)
- *The Baltimore Sun* (1837–present)
- *The Brooklyn Eagle* (1841–1955)
- *Phoenix* (1859–1861)

Contemporary Online Death Notices

Just as news has increasingly gone online, the same has happened with death notices. Whereas in the past, people read the death announcements in their newspaper, now these notices are mostly available online although the traditional method of publishing in the newspaper is still used.

These notices are freely searchable, often provide photographs of the deceased, name family members and relationships and inform readers about the date and time of the funeral service and where the interment will take place. There is usually the opportunity to leave a message of condolence on the website too.

The main websites where contemporary death announcements are to be found are as follows:

- RIP **https://rip.ie**. This website covers all Ireland, although the number of listings for Northern Ireland is less than those in the Republic of Ireland.
- Funeral Times **www.funeraltimes.com**. This website covers Northern Ireland.
- Passed Away **www.passedaway.com**. This website covers Northern Ireland. It does not appear to have been updated for some time but if you are searching for a death notice in the more recent past, it may be of help.

Chapter 4

PERIODICALS AND JOURNALS

Irish genealogical societies produce their own newsletters and journals to be distributed to members. In some cases, these journals, or individual articles within them, are available for purchase by non-members. The journals published by the main Irish genealogical societies have been listed below.

A number of other important and useful journals have been published or are still in production. Some have a focus on Irish documentation and manuscripts, such as the Irish Manuscript Commission's *Analecta Hibernica*, while others published by local history or family history societies have articles of interest on Irish ancestors, records, customs and folklore.

This chapter includes the main sources for the journals published by Irish genealogical societies along with tools for tracking down journals and the articles within them.

Genealogical Society of Ireland (GSI) – *Gazette and Journal*
The monthly *Gazette* is freely available to non-members at **http://bit.ly/3vpxbSI** and online editions go back to January 2006.

An index for editions from 2006 is available at the same location which allows you to search by author or description and helpfully, wildcards are allowed.

An archive for editions from 1996 to 2005 is available at **http://bit.ly/3Q2wPe9** and each edition has an index of contents listed.

The more in-depth annual *Journals of the Genealogical Society of Ireland* contain studies of specific families, locations, or search methodology as well as transcripts of original records.

Journals dating back to spring 2000 are available to purchase on GSI's website at **http://bit.ly/3vmFD5c**.

Copies of GSI's Journals from 1992 to 2016 have been made available on Findmypast. These have been indexed; search terms include names, article title, free text, page number and publication year, and are available to view with a subscription.

Irish Family History Society (IFHS) – News Sheet and Journal

Members get the *Irish Family History Journal* which is published annually and a society *News Sheet* published twice each year.

There are some back copies of the *Irish Family History Journal* listed for purchase on the website at **https://ifhs.ie**.

Irish Genealogical Research Society (IGRS) Bulletin and Journal

The IGRS provides a monthly *Bulletin* to members, containing a summary of genealogy news and new document releases.

The Society's annual journal, *The Irish Genealogist*, has been published since 1937 and its contents include family histories and transcriptions from sources such as newspapers, parish registers, family Bibles, genealogies, voters lists, pedigrees, membership rolls, deeds, marriage settlements, census substitutes, land and tenure surveys, marriage licence bonds, court records, wills, etc.

The Irish Genealogist database, 1937–2001, which comprises a quarter of a million personal names published in the annual journal between 1937 and 2001 may be accessed at **http://bit.ly/3k4eH85**. There are plans to bring the database up to date by 2023.

Members and non-members may purchase individual articles within the journals and also full back copies of *The Irish Genealogist*. Some articles are freely available such as all those within Vol. 10 Nos 1–4. A few of the articles of interest within that volume are:

- A list of Huguenot Pupils at the Hospital and Free School of King Charles II in Dublin
- Scully Tombstones on the Rock of Cashel
- Some Spanish Terrys of Irish Origin
- The Powers of Curraghmore, Co. Waterford: Their Origins and History

Also available to purchase is a collection of family histories published in *The Irish Genealogist*.

Further details may be found at **www.irishancestors.ie/irish-genealogist-contents**.

North of Ireland Family History Society (NIFHS) – NIFHS News and North Irish Roots

NIFHS provides a monthly digital newsletter, *NIFHS News*, to members.

The society's journal, *North Irish Roots*, was first published in 1984 and is currently published twice per year: **www.nifhs.org/resources/north-**

irish-roots. Back copies may be viewed in person at the NIFHS library and some are available to purchase in the online shop: **www.nifhs.org/shop**.

In November 2022, volunteers completed a project that indexed key articles from the NIFHS journals. The resultant PDF *Guide to the Contents of the North Irish Roots Journals 1984–2021* is a members' resource and is searchable by name, place or subject.

One of the benefits of NIFHS membership is access to JSTOR'S Irish Collection (see below for further information). Back copies of *North Irish Roots* are freely available to members via their JSTOR access although there is a 'moving wall' which means that the issues of the most recent three years will not yet be available online.

A fifty-page *Index of Articles in Genealogical Journals* is freely available on the NIFHS website – this lists articles within journals from across Ireland held in the NIFHS library at Newtownabbey and provides their library reference: **http://bit.ly/3ZmcG7i**.

Ulster Historical Foundation (UHF) Familia and Directory of Irish Family History Research

The UHF's Guild was established in 1978 to provide a forum for the Irish and Scots-Irish genealogical community. Guild members receive two annual journals:

- *Familia: Ulster Genealogical Review* – first published in 1985.
- *Directory of Irish Family History Research*. Contains articles of interest as well as providing an opportunity for members to share their research interests with other members.

Guild members can access past articles from both publications on the members' area of the UHF website.

Non-members can purchase copies of both publications on the UHF's book publishing arm, Books Ireland at **www.booksireland.org.uk**.

Other Genealogical and Local History Societies

The Council of Irish Genealogical Organisations (CIGO) was formed in 1992 and is a lobby body for various national and international organisations who share an interest in Irish genealogical research.

It has a list of constituent members from Ireland and overseas, some of which may be helpful for your research and may produce newsletters or journals of interest: **www.cigo.ie/constituent-organisations**.

The Federation of Local History Societies (FLHS) is an umbrella organisation representing over 100 local history and genealogical organisations from the Republic of Ireland. Its website, **www.localhistory.ie**, lists the member organisations and also has back copies of newsletters and journals freely available.

The Federation of Ulster Local Studies (FULS) **www.fuls.org.uk** was set up promote and assist with the study and recording of the history, antiquities and folk-life of Ulster and to develop co-operation and communication between local groups. Federation member organisations are listed and back issues of the newsletter are freely available on its website.

Irish Lives Remembered Magazine

The Irish Family History Centre based in Dublin is a commercial organisation that offers commissioned research. It produces a free digital magazine, *Irish Lives Remembered*, a few times each year. The magazine contains special feature articles, book extracts and regular columns such as 'Dear Genie', which provides help with research blocks, and Photodective where a family photo is analysed.

Current and back editions may be viewed at **www.irishfamilyhistorycentre.com/irish-lives-remembered**.

Irish Roots Magazine

This magazine is published four times per year with the option of a hard copy or a digital copy downloaded to your chosen device upon payment of a subscription. It is possible to purchase single copies or an annual subscription. More details are on the website: **www.irishrootsmedia.com**.

National Library of Ireland (NLI) Sources Database

The NLI has a database for Irish research that contains over 180,000 catalogue records for Irish manuscripts and for articles in Irish periodicals. The database includes:

- All of the NLI's manuscripts catalogued up to the 1980s
- Irish manuscripts held in other libraries and archives in Ireland and worldwide, listed between the 1940s and the 1970s
- Articles, reviews and other content that appeared in over 150 Irish periodicals up to 1969

A list of the periodicals that have been indexed may be found at **http://bit.ly/3vW7g5f**.

The article record gives details of the author, the title and the citation, as well as information about how to access the periodicals in the NLI or in other locations such as online sources or libraries.

Copies of any periodical articles held by the NLI can be ordered through its copying service, using the citation details (including page numbers) and the call number given in the records. More information about the copying service may be found at **www.nli.ie/collections/using-our-collections/copying-services**.

Royal Irish Academy – Irish History Online

Irish History Online (IHO), **www.ria.ie/irish-history-online**, is the national bibliography of Irish history which is hosted and managed by the Royal Irish Academy (RIA). The catalogue comprises publications written about Irish history from earliest times to the present and it lists works on Irish history published since the 1930s, with some earlier material.

Search on the catalogue and then click on each result for further information about the publication, author and where the article may be found.

JSTOR

JSTOR is a digital library that provides access to more than 12 million journal articles, books, images, and primary sources in 75 disciplines.

It has a very good Irish collection that includes seventy-four different titles – a selection of the titles within this collection are:

- *All Ireland Review*
- *Analecta Hibernica*
- *Archaeology Ireland*
- *Archivium Hibernicum*
- *The Belfast Monthly Magazine*
- *The Canadian Journal of Irish Studies*
- *The Catholic Layman*
- *Clogher Record*
- *Dublin Historical Record*
- *The Dublin Penny Journal*
- *History Ireland*
- *Irish Historical Studies*
- *Studia Hibernica*
- *The Irish Penny Journal*
- *The Journal of Irish Archaeology*
- *The Journal of the Royal Society of Antiquaries of Ireland*
- *North Irish Roots*
- *Ulster Journal of Archaeology*

In addition to written material, JSTOR also provides images, many of which can be used without copyright restrictions. These include portraits, political cartoons, views of buildings and scenery, maps and posters. These may be a useful addition to illustrate a family history book or talk.

Two of the images from JSTOR'S images collection are reproduced here:

A vaccination station in Connaught, Ireland. The Graphic, 18 December 1880. (Courtesy of JSTOR and National Library of Medicine)

Royal Charter School, Clontarf, Dublin. (Courtesy of the Wellcome Collection at JSTOR)

JSTOR can be accessed in different ways:

- There is free access to a range of content. Register for a free personal account and you will be able to read online 100 free access articles per month.
- Purchase an individual subscription known as a JPASS – monthly and annual plans are available that allow you to read unlimited articles online and download 120 articles.
- Access is also available via institutions such as schools, colleges, libraries, museums and societies, so it is well worth checking if your family history society, local library or archive provides institutional access. Access to the Irish collection is a membership perk of the NIFHS and other societies or organisations may have a similar arrangement.

Periodical Source Index (PERSI)

PERSI is a subject index for over 10,000 genealogy and local history periodicals that has been produced by the staff of The Genealogy Center of the Allen County Public Library (ACPL) in Fort Wayne, Indiana. This free resource provides more than 3 million citations to readily available periodical sources dating back to 1800. PERSI may be found at **www.genealogycenter.info/persi**.

It is possible to search PERSI on subject, family name, by location or by publication. Alternatively, you can filter by country and county to see what subjects are available. For example, there are 780 articles within the subject of schools that have been published in Ireland and it is possible to filter your results further within this search.

Once you have found an article you are interested in, there are options for finding or accessing the article in question:

- Contact the publisher of the article.
- Do a search to see if it is freely available online. For example, you may find it on the Internet Archive, JSTOR or Google Library.
- Search for the article using WorldCat – see below.
- Order the article from ACPL. It is worth noting that the same nominal fee applies for six articles ordered on the same form plus a small cost per page copied. That being the case, check the PERSI catalogue to see if there are any other articles you would like to order at the same time. Do be aware that ACPL says it can take six to eight weeks to complete orders.

A useful video has been produced by Lisa Louise Cooke featuring Allison Singleton from the Allen County Library, which provides an overview of how to get the best out of your PERSI searches. The video is on YouTube at **http://bit.ly/3isUUi8**.

It is always worthwhile checking back with PERSI on a regular basis as new articles are being indexed on an ongoing basis.

WorldCat

WorldCat is a free research tool that enables you to find items in libraries throughout the world – books, magazines, genealogical records, journals, research theses, maps, etc. It may be found at **www.worldcat.org**.

You can search on a subject such as family name, place name, type of record or for a specific article you may have found in a search on NLI's Sources Database or PERSI.

Once you have found an item of interest, you can check which libraries near you have it or there may be a link to where it is available online.

A guide on how to use WorldCat for genealogy research may be found at **www.worldcat.org/topics/genealogy**.

Libraries Ireland and Libraries NI

If you have a membership of either of these organisations, you will be able to access free e-magazines and newspapers. Note that you need to be resident in the relevant country to qualify for membership. Titles are also available to view during in-person visits.

Libraries Ireland: **www.librariesireland.ie**
Libraries NI: **www.librariesni.org.uk**

Chapter 5

BIOGRAPHIES AND GENEALOGIES

Biographies provide in-depth information on Irish people who have gained prominence in politics, the arts, academia, science, sports, the military, etc. The nobility and landed gentry are the subject of many books that record their origins and ancestry along with coats of arms; their popularity is evidenced by the number of revisions and reprints published.

Many of these works are available online as well as in physical form in libraries and archives. A useful source of links to online books is at the Free Irish Genealogy e-books website **www.irishnobility.blogspot.com**, while a search on WorldCat **www.worldcat.org** will provide information about where both hard copy and digitised versions are to be found.

The most useful publications are covered in this chapter.

Ryan's Biographia Hibernica, 1821

Richard Ryan's *Biographica Hibernica: A Biographical Dictionary of the Worthies of Ireland* was first published in 1819 and it was the first general Irish biographical dictionary.

A second edition in two volumes was published in 1821 and both are freely available on Google Books.

- Volume 1 covers A-C: **http://bit.ly/3Jj1h2C**
- Volume 2 covers C-Y and has an index at the back: **http://bit.ly/402n44q**

Wills, Lives of Illustrious and Distinguished Irishmen from the Earliest Times to the Present Period, 1840–1847

James Wills published six volumes of the *Lives of Illustrious and Distinguished Irishmen from the Earliest Times to the Present Period*. Each volume is laid out in eras with biographies in political, ecclesiastical and literary themes. Each work is freely available at Internet Archive:

- Volume 1, 1840 – **http://bit.ly/3JhtAy8**
- Volume 2, 1840 – **http://bit.ly/402peRA**
- Volume 3, 1841 – **http://bit.ly/402Uv71**
- Volume 4, 1842 – **http://bit.ly/3Rgbyi0**
- Volume 5, 1844 – **http://bit.ly/3R6eDB7**
- Volume 6, 1847 – **http://bit.ly/3wyqbDO**

Wills and Wills, The Irish Nation: Its History and its Biography, 1871–1875
Following the death of his father, Freeman Wills produced a revised version of the *Lives Illustrious and Distinguished Irishmen*, this time with the title of *The Irish Nation: Its History and its Biography*. Issued in four volumes between 1871 and 1875, the fourth volume included mid-nineteenth century figures missing from the original works by James Wills.

Richard 1st Earl of Cork from Vol 2 of Wills and Wills, The Irish Nation … 1860, Edinburgh. (Courtesy of Internet Archive)

There are some very good plates in these books, such the portrait of Richard, 1st Earl of Cork found in Volume 2. These books are all freely available at Internet Archive:

- Volume 1, 1871 – **http://bit.ly/3WEEJfB**
- Volume 2, 1871 – **http://bit.ly/3DgnDO8**
- Volume 3, 1873 – **http://bit.ly/3kJMF1R**
- Volume 4, 1875 – **http://bit.ly/3HdJNBN**

Webb's A Compendium of Irish Biography, 1878

Alfred Webb's 600-page tome published in 1878 is packed with information about people in Irish history. There is a handy index at the front of the book and a list of sources at the back. The brief entry for Adam Duff O'Toole reveals a horrible end in 1327. The book is freely available at Internet Archive at **http://bit.ly/3DeZqYu**.

Adam Duff O'Toole in Webb, A., A Compendium of Irish Biography. (Courtesy of Internet Archive)

Dictionary of National Biography (DNB), 1885–1900

The DNB is a work of reference with articles on more than 29,000 notable figures from British history. It was originally published in sixty-three volumes between 1885 and 1900 by Smith, Elder & Co.

Although it does not have an Irish focus, it does include notable individuals born in Ireland, such as Roger O'Connor (1762–1834), an Irish nationalist who was born at Connorville, County Cork, the son of Roger Connor of Connorville and his wife Anne Longfield. Following his education at Dublin University, the younger Roger joined the English bar in 1784. He entered the Muskerry yeomanry and helped to hunt down Whiteboys but later changed his views and joined the United Irishmen. The entry describes his adventures – imprisonment, elopement, trial for holding up a coach, and subsequent trial and acquittal.

This edition of DNB is freely available at Wikisource: **http://bit.ly/3vUSCv6**.

DNB, 1901 Supplement
The three-volume 1901 Supplement to the DNB 1885–1900, covers subjects who had died between 1885 and 1900 or were otherwise excluded from the original publication. The supplements added notable figures up to the death of Queen Victoria on 22 January 1901; corrections were added in 1904.

This edition is freely available on Wikisource: **http://bit.ly/3GSj66O**.

DNB, second edition 1908–1909
In 1908 and 1909, a revised second edition of DNB was published. The twenty-two volumes are available individually on Google Books and Internet Archive. See Chapter Nine for further information on these online libraries.

The Online Books page hosted by Pennsylvania University has provided hyperlinks to each of the volumes in the second edition at **http://bit.ly/3GzKjd0**.

DNB, 1912 Supplement
The three-volume 1912 Supplement to the second edition of the DNB is freely available at Wikisource: **http://bit.ly/3Quob8A**.

O'Donoghue, The geographic distribution of Irish ability, 1906
The geographic distribution of Irish ability, by D.J. O'Donoghue, Dublin, 1906 is a biographical dictionary of 2,700 Irish men and women, arranged in thirty-two chapters, one for each county in Ireland. Currently, this book is not available online but a hard copy may be tracked down through a search on WorldCat.

Pike's New Century Series, 1898–1912
W.T. Pike edited a number of topographical dictionaries and contemporary biographies. Most of the works were for areas in England, Wales and Scotland although three were contemporary biographies for areas of Ireland.

- *Pike's Dublin and County Dublin Contemporary Biographies*, Dublin, 1908 contains about 450 entries. It is not currently available online but a hard copy may be found through WorldCat.

- *Pike's Ulster Contemporary Biographies*, London, 1909 contains about 1,000 entries. It is not currently available online but a hard copy may be found through WorldCat.
- *Pike's Contemporary Biographies of Cork*, Brighton, 1911, contains about 525 entries, many with photographs. This has been digitised and is freely available on Cork City Libraries Past and Present page at **www.corkcitylibraries.ie/en/cork-past-and-present**.

Thom's Irish Who's Who, 1923

Alexander Thom and Co is best known for its *Dublin City and County Directories*. It ventured into biographical notices with the 1923 *Irish Who's Who* which contains 2,500 names.

As this publication was produced only two years after the creation of the Irish Free State and just a year after the cessation of the Civil War in Ireland, it contains listings for people who were instrumental in the formation of the Irish Free State. Some of the names of interest from this period include Michael Collins, Éamon de Valera and William Cosgrove.

This publication may be accessed with a subscription at Findmypast in the Directories and Social History records collection.

It is also freely available at Wikisource: **http://bit.ly/3QwKx9J** and at Internet Archive: **http://bit.ly/3wcsnAN**.

Crone's A Concise Dictionary of Irish Biography, 1928

This book lives up to its title with brief entries for each person and it is freely available at Internet Archive: **http://bit.ly/401EgHr**.

It was revised with additional entries in 1937 although that version is not available online yet. A copy may be located by searching on WorldCat.

Dictionary of Irish Biography (DIB)

The DIB is a project of the Royal Irish Academy (RIA) which was launched in 2009. It tells the island's life story through the biographies, at home and overseas, of prominent men and women born in Ireland, north and south, and the noteworthy Irish careers of those born outside Ireland.

The chronological scope of the DIB extends from the earliest times to the twenty-first century, although the living are not included. Biographies range in length from 200 to 15,000 words, covering a diverse range of figures.

As an example, the DIB biography of Aengus Fanning (1944–2012), newspaper editor, runs to 1,963 words, describing his parents, time at school, early career, family life and controversial editorship of the *Sunday Independent*. The style and content under Aengus's editorship is described as 'gossip, weighty analysis, and a respectable number of scoops. He aimed at evoking indignation and sardonic amusement as much as approval, and targeted distinguished public figures (and media rivals) for vitriolic denigration.'

The DIB contains nearly 11,000 lives and it is regularly updated. It is freely available online at **www.dib.ie** while the print version consists of eleven volumes published by Cambridge University Press.

Dictionary of Ulster Biography

Provided by the Ulster History Circle, this is a database of over 2,000 free-to-access biographies of people from the nine counties of Ulster who have made a significant contribution to the region: **www.newulsterbiography.co.uk**.

The Ulster History Circle also erects blue plaques in public places to honour those who have contributed to the Province's history and they are listed on the same website.

Burke's Genealogical Series

The DIB includes an entry on the Burke family who published pedigree and genealogical books. John Burke (1786–1848) was an Irish genealogist who founded the celebrated genealogical series. His first genealogical book, *A General and Heraldic Dictionary of the Peerage and Baronetage of the United Kingdom* (1826), was the first of its type to be arranged alphabetically and to treat peers and baronets together. From 1847 onwards, it was published annually and became known as *Burke's Peerage*.

From c.1840, John was assisted by his son, John Bernard Burke (1814–1892), who was later knighted and appointed Ulster King of Arms. After his father's death, Sir John Bernard compiled, edited and revised the Burke publications. He, however, was castigated by his contemporaries for his uncritical acceptance of doubtful pedigrees and repeated inaccuracies which were made more serious because of his official position, although more recent editions have been checked for accuracy and rewritten.

Burke's publications where people of Irish birth or descent are recorded include:

- A general and heraldic dictionary of the peerage and baronetage of the United Kingdom
- A genealogical and heraldic history of the commoners of Great Britain and Ireland, later issued as a genealogical and heraldic dictionary of the landed gentry of Great Britain and Ireland
- A general and heraldic dictionary of the peerages of England, Ireland and Scotland, extinct, dormant and in abeyance
- The knightage of Great Britain and Ireland
- A general armoury of England, Scotland and Ireland later retitled *Encyclopaedia of Heraldry*
- Heraldic illustrations, comprising the armorial bearings of the principal families of the empire with pedigrees and annotations
- A genealogical and heraldic history of the landed gentry of Ireland
- *Irish Family Records* (1976)

Out-of-copyright editions are to be found freely available in the online libraries Hathi Trust, Google Books, Internet Archive and Open Library (see Chapter Nine) while a search of WorldCat will provide links to online versions.

Some are available on Ancestry and this includes the more recent *Irish Family Records* while My Heritage **www.myheritage.com** and Findmypast also have a small selection; these may be viewed with a subscription.

More recent editions may be viewed with a subscription on the Burke's Peerage website **www.burkespeerage.com** or in libraries.

Cokayne's Pedigrees

George Edward Cokayne (1825–1911) was a genealogist and herald at the College of Arms whose work was regarded as more detailed and scholarly than Burke's. The works which were revised and updated and contain mention of Irish born or of Irish descent include:

- Complete Peerage of England, Scotland, Ireland, Great Britain and the United Kingdom Extant, Extinct, or Dormant
- Complete Baronage

These are freely available at Internet Archive **www.archive.org**.

O'Hart's Pedigrees

John O'Hart (1824–1902) was an Irish teacher, antiquarian and genealogist who produced two key works of pedigrees:

Irish Pedigrees; or the Origin and Stem of the Irish Nation
First published in 1876 in two volumes with further editions and reprints, this is intriguing for tracing the ancient Irish families back to the mythological Milesian invaders and indeed, back to Adam.

While this aspect of O'Hart's work is interesting, it is to be taken with a very large pinch of salt. The pedigrees for the modern period, however, are more credible. The books are freely available at Internet Archive:

- Volume 1, 1892 – **http://bit.ly/3DfpdA3**
- Volume 2, 1892 – **http://bit.ly/3DjPNrw**

The Irish landed Gentry when Cromwell came to Ireland, 1887
This has Anglo-Irish pedigrees along with a number of lists of names drawn from historical documents. It is freely available at Internet Archive: **http://bit.ly/3HgonEc**.

Each of these books have a name index at the back.

Edward MacLysaght's Irish families

Edward MacLysaght (1887–1986) was an English-born and of Irish descent author and historian who worked for the Irish Manuscript Commission (IMC) and in 1943 was appointed as the Chief Herald at the Genealogical Office in Dublin Castle. This body took over the work of the Office of Arms which had been managed by the Deputy Ulster King of Arms under the British government. MacLysaght's genealogical and heraldic publications are:

- *Irish Families: Their Names, Arms and Origins* first published in 1957 contains sept arms of Gaelic families and notes on each name, although not all names are included. The third edition, 1972, is freely available on the Open Library and may be borrowed for an hour at a time. Just register for a free account at **http://bit.ly/3HgHDl0**.
- *More Irish families*, 1960, is freely available on Family Search Digital Library at **http://bit.ly/3JkAm6p**.
- *Supplement to Irish families*, 1964 and *The Surnames of Ireland*, 1969, are not currently available online but second-hand copies are often advertised for sale and you may find them in a library by searching WorldCat.

Chapter 6

THE GAZETTE

The London, Edinburgh and Belfast editions

The Gazette, established in 1665, is the official public record of the United Kingdom. It contains official information on individuals and companies in the form of notices published in the record. These notices are still published today.

If your ancestor was made bankrupt, received an honour or award or a military promotion, they will be mentioned here.

The Gazette was published in separate versions in London, Edinburgh and Belfast (the Belfast version was published from 7 June 1921 following the partition of Ireland). It was also published in Dublin – see below. A brief overview of the contents of *The Gazette* is as follows:

Company Profiles:
- Individual company profiles
- Information recorded with Companies House
- Company timelines

Awards and Accreditations:
- Queen's or King's Birthday and New Year Honours
- Military and civilian awards
- Dedicated section on First World War

Wills and Probate:
- Deceased estates notices

Insolvency:
- Corporate insolvency notices
- Personal insolvency notices

The Gazette is free to search and may be found at **www.thegazette.co.uk**.

You can register for a free account and this will allow you to save your searches and specific notices or to create a bespoke edition.

The easiest way to start searching is to go to the All Notices section at **www.thegazette.co.uk/all-notices** and enter your search term into the text box. It is possible to filter by type of notice, notice code, location of event, date of publication and place of publication.

Be aware that there was no standard way of submitting and displaying information. Particularly if you are searching for honours and awards for gallantry and meritorious service in the armed forces, often no first name was used, just the service person's surname and an initial for the first name. However, for soldiers the following information had to be provided:

- Name
- Regiment
- Date
- Regimental service number (pre-1920 service numbers were not fixed and if a soldier changed regiments they would have a new service number assigned to them)
- Service number (1920 onwards)

The Gazette has a dedicated First World War search area at **www.thegazette.co.uk/awards-and-accreditation/ww1**. There is also a section that describes the major medals awarded for gallantry or meritorious service at **www.thegazette.co.uk/awards-and-accreditation/medals**.

The following editions of *The Gazette* are also available at Findmypast with a subscription:

- London Gazette 1665–2018
- Edinburgh Gazette 1797–2018
- Belfast Gazette 1922–2018

Dublin Gazette

King James II established the *Dublin Gazette* in May 1689, but after he was defeated by William III in 1690, its functions were taken over by the *London Gazette.*

One copy survives from the seventeenth century – the edition of 12–29 March 1690 held by The Library Company of Philadelphia. Interestingly, it is an early example of propaganda and 'fake news' that records (falsely) that William's forces abroad had been roundly defeated and the prince expelled from his office of stadtholder. This early edition and some others are part of a digital exhibition on the Beyond 2022 website that may be viewed here: **http://bit.ly/3w0KN7s**.

In 1705, a new *Dublin Gazette* was established and it was published more or less continuously from that date.

The *Dublin Gazette* ceased publication during the Easter Rising and for more than a week following it, with the result that a compendium issue was later published for the period between 25 April and 9 May 1916.

Following the Anglo-Irish Treaty that ushered in partition of Ireland, the final edition was published on 27 January 1922.

There are PDF files for editions of the *Dublin Gazette* from 1750s to 1800, but beware, these are large files and will take some time to download. They may be freely accessed via Wikipedia's the *Dublin Gazette* page at **http://bit.ly/3vV5fGC**.

Editions between 1757 to 1810 (with gaps) are freely available via the historical documents at the online catalogue of the Houses of the Oireachtas (the Irish Parliament). Simply type 'Gazette' into the title search box and it is possible to search for names, places or events within the records. The search function may be found at **http://bit.ly/3X7ejnE**.

There are a small number of *Dublin Gazettes* available on Ireland's Virtual Treasury, the virtual reconstruction of the Public Records Office in Dublin that was destroyed in 1922. It seems that the aim is eventually to create links to all surviving copies at **https://virtualtreasury.ie**.

Editions published between 1750 and 1800 have been indexed and are searchable on Findmypast with a paid subscription.

Irish Bulletin

During the Irish War of Independence (21 January 1919–11 July 1921), *The Gazette* had a rival in the *Irish Bulletin* which was the official newspaper of the first Dáil Éireann government of the Irish Republic. The first Dáil consisted of seventy-three Sinn Féin candidates elected in 1918 who abstained from Westminster and set up their own rival assembly in Dublin.

Through their Department of Propaganda, they published the *Irish Bulletin* on a weekly basis from 11 November 1919 to 11 July 1921. Copies of this publication may be viewed with a subscription at **www.irishnewsarchive.com**.

It is also to be found in hardcopy and microfilm at the National Library of Ireland. See Chapter One for searching in other archives and libraries.

Iris Oifigiúil

On 31 January 1922, the newly created Irish Free State began to publish a new gazette called *Iris Oifigiúil*, sometimes referred to in English as the *Irish State Gazette*.

Iris Oifigiúil is the official Irish State gazette and is published twice a week, in addition to supplements published at various times during the year. It is still the official record of the government of the Republic of Ireland.

Contemporary editions and archived issues dating back to 2002 can be accessed at **www.irisoifigiuil.ie**.

Chapter 7

ALMANACS AND STREET DIRECTORIES

Street directories are a valuable tool for your Irish research as they contain information on the gentry, the professional classes, merchants and farmers.

They record the names and addresses of the local butchers, pawnbrokers, blacksmiths and coach builders as well as places of worship, schools and hotels along with the names of clergy, schoolmasters and bank managers.

The names and addresses of the local Member of Parliament, magistrates, poor law guardians and town commissioners are included in many street directories, along with the names and locations of schools, churches and charitable institutions.

Historical information that provides rich background information about the lives of our ancestors is often provided, such as the main industries in an area, population statistics, taxes levied and the transportation links with other towns.

In towns, people tended to move around more frequently and the directories allow you to trace the movement of families. In rural areas, farming families were more likely to have remained in one place, although small tenant farmers, labourers and servants tend not to be listed in the directories.

Street directories commenced publication in Dublin and at a later stage, we find provincial directories, which were produced for particular cities, regions or counties such as Belfast, Cork, Fermanagh, Munster or Ulster.

Countrywide directories first came into existence in the early nineteenth century with Pigot & Co publications.

The quality and quantity of the information varies greatly and the directories are laid out in different ways.

How to find directories

Many local libraries, archives and family history centres hold good selections of directories in hard copy format, while some are available as microfilm. Yet others have been digitised and made available online, some of which are free and others are available as part of a subscription.

Libraries and Archives

NAI, NLI and PRONI have substantial holdings of street directories that may be viewed in person. PRONI also has an online database of directories.

If you are looking for a directory for a particular area, it is always worth checking with the local archive or library to find out what their holdings are. Local collections can be held in online, hard copy or microfilm formats. Addresses for libraries and archives may be found in the Appendix.

The WorldCat catalogue can be of help to check what is available and in which formats **www.worldcat.org**.

Street directories in the Linen Hall Library, Belfast. (Courtesy of Natalie Bodle)

Findmypast, Ancestry, My Heritage and Family Search all have directory holdings – a paid subscription is required for the first three, but Family Search can be accessed with a free account.

Online libraries such as Google Books, Internet Archive and Hathi Trust also have a range of directories that are free to view.

Portals

Shane Wilson's Directory Database has just over 1,000 links to historic directories of Ireland that are available on free and subscription websites; the database includes directories for purchase on CD or download.

The database, which may be searched for keywords, county or dates, is available at **www.swilson.info/dirdb.php**.

Peter J. Clarke's website also has links to a number of directories at **http://irishalmanacs.blogspot.com**.

Links have been provided for specific directories that are detailed below.

Early Publications

Some of the early books classified as directories provide information about the local landlords, gentry and nobility, and their residences, along with some historical and geographical information. They do not provide the wealth of information found in later publications that we would more readily recognise as directories. However, it may be the case that you will find a mention of your ancestor or of the place where your ancestor lived within these books.

Taylor and Skinner's Road Maps of Ireland

Published in 1778, *Taylor and Skinner's Road Maps of Ireland* has maps showing the roads from one town to another and they are annotated with the seats of the principal inhabitants of the area.

At the back of the book, there is an alphabetical list of the nobility, listed in order of precedence and a list of inhabitants by county, along with the page number of the map showing their residence.

This book is freely available at Internet Archive: **http://bit.ly/3GDcRT1**, at the L. Brown Collection: **http://bit.ly/3H0pDwi** and on Shane Wilson: **http://bit.ly/3ZKDTAS**.

Post-Chaise Companion or Travellers Directory through Ireland

The *Post-Chaise Companion or Travellers Directory through Ireland* was published in 1786. Its introduction opened with:

The public are here presented with a new and accurate description of the roads of Ireland comprised in a neat convenient pocket volume, similar to Mr Patterson's useful book of the English Roads.

Unlike Mr Patterson's work, this book contained descriptions of the towns and mentioned noblemen's and gentlemen's seats with accounts of buildings, antiquities, modern improvements and natural productions.

The book lists the subscribers and goes on to describe Dublin in some length. A description of the road to Drogheda and Donaghadee is provided with the names of inhabitants and interesting historical facts, such as:

> Three miles from Drogheda, at the mouth of the river, is Bewly, a very fine old seat of Mr Montgomery. It was built by Sir Henry Tichborne, afterwards Lord Ferrard.
>
> Four miles from Drogheda on the river is Carter's Town, the seat of Mr Hamlin; and about a mile distant situated at the foot of a hill, is Stonehouse, the seat of Mr Owens.

Various routes are described in a similar manner and a table of distances from town to town is provided, along with an alphabetical index of towns and a map of the roads of Ireland.

This book is freely available at Internet Archive: **http://bit.ly/3iC26bQ**.

Early Almanacs and Directories

Findmypast has partnered with SOG, Dublin City Libraries and the RIA to produce a record set entitled *Ireland, Directories 1636–1799*. These publications were produced during the seventeenth and eighteenth centuries and have been provided as images that may be browsed with a subscription. The publications in this collection are:

- *A New Almanack and Prognostication for the Year of Our Lord*, Patrick True, 1636
- *A New Almanack for the Year of Our Lord*, Patrick Plunket, 1684
- *Advice from the Stars*, John Whalley, 1698
- *Bourke's Almanack*, John Bourke, 1684
- *Dublin Directory (Wilson's)*, 1751–53 and 1760
- List of Dublin Freemen and Freeholders, 1762
- Principal Inhabitants of Dublin, 1684
- *Sydereus Nuncius or an Ephemeris for the Year Human Redemption*, John Whalley, 1686

- *The English Registry,* 1752–53
- *The Gentleman and Citizen's Almanack* (*Watson's*) and *The English Registry and Wilson's Dublin Directory,* 1761–62, 1763–99 with map, 1769–72
- *Vax Urania or an Almanack for the years Human Redemption,* John Whalley, 1685

Dublin Directories

The Treble Almanac and Dublin Directory
The Treble Almanac incorporates three separate publications, bound together, which provide lists of key appointments throughout Ireland, along with a comprehensive list of Dublin inhabitants:

- *John Watson Stewart's Almanac* – information on a range of topics
- Exshaw's English Court Registry – key individuals of the day
- *Wilson's Dublin Directory* – a listing of Dublin streets and merchants

The 1783, 1812, 1818, 1822, 1829 editions are available at Findmypast with a subscription.

Google Books has the 1804 edition at **http://bit.ly/3klbS2s** and the 1815 edition at **http://bit.ly/3w74Fpk**.

The 1822 edition is freely available on Hathi Trust: **http://bit.ly/3kqmGfB**.

The 1832 edition is freely available at Internet Archive: **http://bit.ly/3CUUlED**.

Pettigrew & Oulton, Dublin Almanac and General Register of Ireland
Pettigrew & Oulton began publishing the first detailed annual directory of Dublin in 1834. Updated versions of the *Dublin Almanac and General Register of Ireland* were published throughout the 1830s and 1840s.

The volumes contain typical almanac information such as lists of fair days, dates of eclipses of the sun and moon, important dates, moon phases, tide tables, weights, measures and conversion tables, carriage fares, fair dates, postage rates and towns and reigning European royalty. This is followed by a list of nobility and government officials throughout Ireland, including: key members and office holders of the Constabulary; Coast Guard; Revenue Police; Customs and Excise; Civil Service; Post Office; public bodies; Church leaders; colleges; hospitals; medical practitioners; institutions; societies and clubs; banks; canal and railway companies.

> **THE HOSPITAL FOR THE RELIEF OF POOR LYING-IN WOMEN,**
> *The first of the kind in Her Majesty's dominions, Established by Royal Charter,*
>
> Was opened in George's lane, 25th March, 1745, by the late Bartholomew Mosse, who, with the assistance of several charitable benefactions, supported it for nearly twelve years; and having built the Hospital in Great Britain street, (for which he also obtained a Charter,) the latter was opened for the reception of patients, 8th December, 1757.
>
> The Hospital contains 140 beds, 15 of which are appropriated to the diseases of females.
>
> Delivered in the Hospital from the 8th December, 1757, to the 31st December, 1844, 151,011 women, of 7,952 boys, and 7,376 girls. Two thousand three hundred and forty-two had twins, thirty-two had three, and one, in the year 1788, had four, Total number of children born, 153,228; Children dead, 5,656; still born, 8,974; women dead, 1,804.
>
> Proportion of males and females born, about *twelve* males to *eleven* females.
> Do   Children dying in the hospital, about *one* to *twenty-four*.
> Do   Children still born, about *one* to *seventeen*.
> Do   Women having twins,(and more) about *one* to *sixty*.
> Do   Women dying in child-bed, about *one* to *eighty-nine*.
> Do   Women having three and four children, about *one* to *five thousand*.
>
> Women admitted into the Hospital from 1st January, 1844, to 31st December, 1844, 2,290; delivered, 2165, of 1,198 boys and 1,020 girls; 37 had twins—one had three; children still born, 137; children died, 28; women died, 14.

Entry for the Hospital for the Relief of Poor Lying-In Women in Pettigrew & Oulton's Dublin Almanac and General Register of Ireland. (Courtesy of Google Books)

The official authorities for each county are listed, followed by a record of charitable institutions; a list of the members of the House of Lords and House of Commons; names of the ships of the Royal Navy, along with key members of the armed forces.

This is followed by the *Dublin Directory* with an alphabetical list of the principal inhabitants of the city and suburbs.

Streets are listed with information about where the street extends to and from and the parish in which it is located. There is an alphabetical list of Dublin inhabitants with their occupation and address. Barristers are listed with their date of entry to the Bar, as are attorneys, apothecaries and the clergy of various churches. Next, the inhabitants are listed by street, followed by trades and their practitioners, and the annals of Dublin, which comprises key dates in the history of the city. The following editions of these directories may be found at:

- 1835 – Findmypast and Google Books: **http://bit.ly/3QPGCoA**
- 1841 – Ancestry **www.ancestry.com**
- 1842 – Fáilte Romhat: **www.failteromhat.com**
- 1845 – www.findmypast.co.uk
- 1847 – Google Books: **http://bit.ly/3ZIAz9s**
- 1849 – Google Books: **http://bit.ly/3w8uDZw**

Dublin City Library and Archive

Dublin City Library and Archive has a very good selection of Dublin directories, the earliest of which dates from 1636. It has an almost complete set of Dublin directories from 1751 to the present in hardcopy, which includes:

- *Wilson's Dublin Directories*, 1751–1753; 1761–1837
- *Pettigrew & Oulton's Dublin Directories*, 1834–1847
- *Thom's Irish Almanac and Official Directories*, 1844–present

It also has directories on microfilm dating from 1729 and holds publications that cover areas other than Dublin. A list of its holdings may be found at **http://bit.ly/3H6uD2G**.

Provincial Directories

Provincial directories often provide more detailed local information than could be provided in the countrywide directories.

For example, Smyth and Lyons published Belfast's first street directory: the Belfast Directory for 1807. A further edition was published in 1808 and both of these were published by the UHF in 1991 as a single volume entitled *Merchants in Plenty, Joseph Smyth's Belfast Directories of 1807 and 1808*.

The next directory published for Belfast was Thomas Bradshaw's *Belfast General and Commercial Directory* in 1819; this was followed by Belfast directories published by Matier, Martin and Henderson from the 1830s onwards.

Of course, Belfast was also mentioned in the countrywide directories such as Pigot & Co published from the 1820s. Other towns, cities and provinces in Ireland followed a similar path as far as publication of directories specific to their area.

Cork City Library

Cork City Library has a website called Cork Past and Present **https://digital.corkpastandpresent.com**, which provides information of interest to the genealogist, including street directories. The earliest of these is *McDonnell's Cork City Directory for 1753* and the latest is the 1945 *Paramount Cork City and County Official Directory and Almanac*.

These records, which are freely available, are searchable by name or place – or you can browse the directories.

Irish Genealogical Research Society (IGRS)

The IGRS currently has four directories on its website that are freely available to non-members at **www.irishancestors.ie/unique-resources**. The directories are:

- Cork Directory, 1787
- Cork City Stallholders, 1845–2005

- Dublin Directory, 1775
- Dublin Directory, 1803

Lennon Wylie

The Lennon Wylie website at **www.lennonwylie.co.uk** has transcribed copies of Belfast and Ulster publications from 1805 to 1970. These are freely available and searchable by name and place or you can simply browse.

PRONI

PRONI has indexed and scanned a number of directories for Belfast and Ulster including Bradshaw's 1819 Directory. A list of the directories available is at **www.nidirect.gov.uk/articles/about-street-directories**.

The directories may be searched for free at **https://streetdirectories.proni.gov.uk** and it is possible to filter by directory and year.

UHF

The UHF has indexed a number of street directories for Ulster and some for Tipperary which have been made available on its online databases; access is for members only at **www.ancestryireland.com**.

Ancestry collection

Ancestry has indexed directories in its Ireland, City and Regional Directories, 1836–1947 collection – there are nearly 12 million records available to view with a subscription at **www.ancestry.com**.

Provincial directories at Findmypast

Findmypast has a very good selection of provincial directories in its Directories and Social History record set. These have been indexed and the original page can be viewed. The directories available are listed below and these give a flavour of the type of directory generally available.

Basset produced a number of county directories although they were in a small number and they never covered the whole country:

- *George Basset's Limerick City and County and Principal Towns in the Counties of Clare, Tipperary and Kerry, 1881*
- *George Basset's Kilkenny City and County Guide and Directory, 1884*
- *George Basset's Wexford County Guide and Directory, 1885*
- *George Basset's County Down Guide and Directory, 1886*
- *George Basset's Louth County Guide and Directory, 1886*

- *George Basset's The Book of County Armagh, 1888*
- *George Basset's The Book of Antrim, 1888*

Matier's Belfast Directory, 1835–6
This covers the city of Belfast and Ballymacarrett. Along with inhabitants, it includes noblemen, gentry, professionals, merchants and traders.

Henderson's Belfast Directory, 1850
This has approximately 16,000 names – it focuses mainly on Belfast with some information on the surrounding villages and County Antrim.

James Alexander Henderson, The Belfast and Province of Ulster Directory for 1856.
This directory was first published from the offices of the *Belfast Newsletter* in 1852, and 1856 was the third edition. Both directories contain extensive information about Belfast as well as covering each of the nine counties of Ulster. Descriptions are provided for each county along with a street directory for Belfast and Ballymacarratt, an alphabetical list of Belfast inhabitants, a trade directory for the towns and villages of Ulster and a list of the administrative and military positions for each county.

Macloskie's Directory of Fermanagh, 1848
This was published during the Great Famine and has a detailed description of the county. It lists the inhabitants of Enniskillen along with the smaller towns of Lisnaskea, Brookeborough, Maguiresbridge, Belleek, Garrison, etc.

The King's County Directory, 1890
This directory was published by the *King's County Chronicle* (now known as County Offaly). In addition to lists of local inhabitants, it includes lists of guardians, ratepayers and municipal voters.

Ashe's Limerick and Clare Directory, 1891–1892
This is one of a small number of directories that dealt with Limerick and Clare before the twentieth century, which makes it particularly valuable.

Guy's Limerick Directory, 1912
This directory has a comprehensive listing for business, public bodies, religious and educational establishments as well as a listing of the postal and telegraph services in Ireland. There are a number of advertisements for local businesses.

Tempest's Jubilee Annual, 1909 – Louth

This was an anniversary edition that included biographies of notable people and a directory of businesses in the county. One of the biographies was for Mr John Charles Duffy who was born on 15 January 1830, the son of Charles Duffy, a prominent merchant who died from typhoid in 1840 aged 36. He and Mr Patrick Wynne started the Dublin Street Brewery. John Charles married a French woman and left two sons (who had since died) and two daughters. One was married to Mr Paul Brown of Carlow and the other to Mr O'Meara of Dublin. A niece, Miss Brennan, was married to Mr John Quin, JP of Dromin. Mr Duffy died in 1860.

Henry & Coughlan's General Directory of Cork and Munster, 1867

This contains a general directory for Cork city and also *Wynne's Directory of the Province of Munster*. Each county in the province, i.e. Clare, Cork, Kerry, Limerick, Tipperary and Waterford, has a list of administrative and judicial officers along with a full trade directory for each town.

Guy's Directory of Munster, 1893

This covers the province of Munster, which contains counties Clare, Cork, Kerry, Limerick, Tipperary and Waterford.

Sligo Chronicle Almanac and Directory, 1878 and 1889

This was published by the *Sligo Chronicle* newspaper and contains a wealth of information about County Sligo and its inhabitants. There are comprehensive lists of officials and institutions, along with history of the county.

Shearman's Directory of Waterford, Kilkenny and the Southeast, 1839

This is one of the earliest local directories published in Ireland and the first that focused on the south-east. The main towns included are Waterford, Kilkenny, Clonmel, Carrick-on-Suir, New Ross, Carlow and Tramore. Along with an alphabetical list of inhabitants, there is also a trades and professional directory, plus lists of government and administrative post holders and information about institutions such as schools, colleges and churches.

Harvey's Waterford Almanac and Directory, 1866

This includes local information for the city of Waterford, a calendar of local events, fairs and markets, trades and professional listings and an alphabetical directory of residents as well as a map of the city.

My Heritage Collection

My Heritage has a number of provincial directories that are available with a subscription at **www.myheritage.com**.

- *Henderson's 1856 Ulster Directory*
- *Henry & Coughlan's General Directory of Cork and Munster, 1867*
- *Basset's Limerick, Clare, Tipperary and Kerry Directory, 1880–81*
- *Basset's County Down Guide and Directory, 1886*
- *Basset's Book of County Armagh, 1888*
- *Basset's Book of Antrim, 1888*
- *Basset's Wexford County Guide and Directory, 1885*
- *Basset's Kilkenny Guide and Directory, 1884*
- *Basset's Louth Guide and Directory, 1886*
- *Francis Guy's County and City of Cork Directory, 1875–76*

Post Office Directories

There are a few surviving city specific directories available online.

- *Post Office Belfast Annual Directory 1843–44* is freely available at Google Books: **http://bit.ly/3GOG5ym**.
- *Post Office Cork Directory 1845* is freely available at Cork Archives at **http://bit.ly/3GKlsn7**.
- *Post Office Dublin Annual Directory and Calendar* for 1843 and 1858 is available on Findmypast with a subscription.
- *Post Office Dublin Directory and Calendar* for 1918 in three volumes is freely available at Family Search:
  - Volume 1 – **http://bit.ly/3w802v9**
  - Volume 2 – **http://bit.ly/3IUt6xK**
  - Volume 3 – **http://bit.ly/3wbzjOi**

Countrywide Directories

Leet's Directory

Leet's Directory to the Noted Places, and Gentlemen's Seats in Ireland was first published in 1812 with a second edition in 1814. The second edition commences with an alphabetical list of place names in Ireland, providing the nearest post town, the county and the chief resident (usually the local landowner) or a description if it is, for example, the name of a townland.

Next is an alphabetical index of names cross-referenced with the page number for their residence. A list of post towns in England, Wales and Scotland along with the cost of postage for a single letter from Dublin,

Waterford or Donaghadee is provided. Unlike today where the cost of postage throughout the United Kingdom is fixed, no matter which town the letter is being sent to, we find different rates applied in 1814. The cost of posting a letter to Gateshead in England cost 1s 2d from Dublin and Donaghadee but 1s 4d from Waterford.

Although there are 8,800 names in this book, the information on them is scanty, but it may help you to narrow down a location of where your ancestor was to be found in the early nineteenth century.

Leet's second edition is available with a subscription at Findmypast within the Directories and Social History record set.

It is also freely available on Google Books at **http://bit.ly/3ZzICoY**.

Pigot & Co

Pigot & Co produced a Commercial Directory of Scotland, Ireland and the four most northern counties of England for 1820–21 and 1822.

In it, the Irish section runs to 248 pages. It starts with Dublin providing an overview of the city, its geography, history, public buildings, charitable institutions, places of worship, trade and commerce and adjacent country. Dublin Castle is described in the directory as:

> adjacent to the Royal Exchange, is supposed to have been built about the year 1205. In the reign of King John, it was considered a place of great strength. Queen Elizabeth [the First] established it as the seat of government. Before that time the Governor's Courts were held at Kilmainham and other places, the Castle had been the residence of the Lord Lieutenants of Ireland since the year 1563, who are entitled to a salary of £30,000 a year by parliament. This building is very extensive and has had many recent additions and improvements; it has an armoury for 80,000 men. Attached to the Castle is a new and beautiful Chapel of most exquisite architecture, the interior or which is superb in the extreme, divine service is performed there in public every Sunday at 12 noon.

Next, information about key staff in the Post Office and postage rates are provided. An alphabetical list of nobility and gentry of Dublin with their addresses comes next followed by Merchants and Tradesmen listed alphabetically by trade, such as Academies; Accountants; Agricultural Implement Makers; Agents Ship and Commercial; Anchor Smiths; Apothecaries; Architects and Builders; and so on.

This is followed by a list of public institutions and their addresses such as Alms Houses; Asylums; Places of Worship; Goals and Penitentiaries (15 of these); Hospitals; Theatres; Police Offices; Courts; etc.

The departure and return to Dublin of mail and post coaches to various towns is recorded. We learn for example, that the post coach to Armagh departs from Gosson's Hotel at 6 Bolton Street, Dublin every Sunday, Tuesday and Thursday at six in the morning through Drogheda, Dundalk and Newtownhamilton. It returns every Monday, Wednesday and Friday at six in the evening.

Benchers and Barristers with their date of admission are listed along with Attorneys with the court to which they belong.

The Dublin section finishes with an alphabetical list of those named in the preceding pages.

Following the Dublin Directory, there are alphabetical listings for the main towns in Ireland. A brief summary is provided of the town with a listing of the names and addresses of the main trades. The larger towns such as Belfast and Cork also have an alphabetical index of names at the end of their section.

This edition is freely available at Internet Archive: **http://bit.ly/3w16dBa**.

The second edition appeared in 1824 as the *City of Dublin and Hibernian Provincial Directory* and is referred to as the first comprehensive commercial directory of Ireland ever published.

It is organised by province with towns and villages listed alphabetically – over 220 urban centres are listed along with the key office holders, gentry, professionals, tradesmen, schools, institutions, churches and pubs in the general area.

The 1824 edition is available with a subscription from Findmypast.

Pigot's 1824 Directory of Ireland is available at My Heritage with a subscription.

Slater's Directories

Isaac Slater was a partner of James Pigot from 1840; he eventually took over the publication of Pigot's directories with his *National Commercial Directory of Ireland* in 1846.

Slater's directories were laid out in much the same way as Pigot's with expanded lists of inhabitants of the area that included the surrounding villages. Each subsequent edition provided greater information.

The 1846 edition is freely available on Google Books at **http://bit.ly/3w1z6xm**. It can also be accessed with a subscription at Findmypast.

By 1870, the title had changed to *Slater's Royal National Commercial Directory of Ireland* and further editions were published in 1881 and 1894. These are also available on Findmypast.

Slater's directories for 1824, 1856, 1881 and 1894 may be accessed at My Heritage with a subscription.

Thom's Directories

Thom's directories are often regarded as Dublin directories but they do contain countrywide information. *Thom's Irish Almanac and Official Directory* was first published in 1844 by Alexander Thom and updated on an annual basis. They were printed with various titles:

- *Thom's Irish Almanac and Official Directory*
- *Thom's Official Directory of the United Kingdom of Great Britain and Ireland*
- *Thom's Official Directory of Ireland*
- *Thom's Directory of Ireland*
- *Thom's Commercial Directory*

The 1850 edition of *Thom's Irish Almanac and Official Directory* included:

- A British, colonial and parliamentary directory
- Statistics of Ireland
- Ecclesiastical directory
- Law directory
- Banking directory
- Postal and conveyance directory
- County directory
- Borough directory
- Post Office Dublin City and County Directory

The county directories provide geographic, manufacturing and statistical information along with information about institutions such as the hospitals, banks, workhouses, police, coast guard, military barracks, etc.

This is followed by the names of the Lord Lieutenant; the High Sheriff; Deputy Lieutenants; Magistrates; County Officers; Stamp Distributors; Barony Cess Collectors; Inspectors of Weights and Measures; Militia Staff; Constabulary Officers; Coast Guard Stations; Manor courts; Petty Sessions Courts; Board of Superintendence of Prisons; Bridewells and Keepers; County Infirmary at Lisburn staff; District Lunatic Asylum at Belfast staff; medical officers of fever hospitals and dispensaries; poor law unions and dates of fairs.

A borough directory provides additional information for the larger towns and cities such as Armagh, Bandon, Belfast, Cashel, Drogheda, Ennis, Galway, etc. These detail more information about the borough and list further names connected with banks, post offices, courts, banks, hotels and institutions.

Some of the County Carlow officials listed in Thom's 1850 Irish Almanac. (Courtesy Hathi Trust)

Thom's was updated on an annual basis with its final publication in 2013.

Findmypast has a number of Thom's directories available to view while Ancestry has the 1904 edition – both require a subscription.

The following directories are to be found on Google Books, Internet Archive and Hathi Trust:

- 1850 – *Thom's Irish Almanac and Official Directory* – Hathi Trust: **http://bit.ly/3QS2pMo**
- 1851 – *Thom's Irish Almanac and Official Directory* – Google Books: **http://bit.ly/3IUxU6w**
- 1852 – *Thom's Irish Almanac and Official Directory* – Google Books: **http://bit.ly/3QMuBQG**
- 1857 – *Thom's Irish Almanac and Official Directory* – Google Books: **http://bit.ly/3kncFQz**
- 1859 – *Thom's Almanac and Official Directory* – Google Books: **http://bit.ly/3w9tWiE**

- 1870 – *Thom's Irish Almanac and Official Directory* – Hathi Trust: **http://bit.ly/3ZU5Xlt**
- 1873 – *Thom's Irish Almanac and Official Directory* – Google Books: **http://bit.ly/3iJR5VT**
- 1874 – *Thom's Irish Almanac and Official Directory* – Google Books: **http://bit.ly/3kaRjWj**
- 1876 – *Thom's Irish Almanac and Official Directory* – Google Books: **http://bit.ly/3iCzlvK**
- 1878 – *Thom's Irish Almanac and Official Directory* – Google Books: **http://bit.ly/3kkBlcj**
- 1881 – *Thom's Official Directory of the United Kingdom of Great Britain and Ireland* – Google Books: **http://bit.ly/3QSDQ1J**
- 1883 – *Thom's Official Directory of the United Kingdom of Great Britain and Ireland* – Google Books: **http://bit.ly/3iD2B5z**
- 1884 – *Thom's Official Directory of the United Kingdom of Great Britain and Ireland* – Internet Archive: **http://bit.ly/3ZENE3s**

Ask About Ireland
AskAboutIreland.ie and the Cultural Heritage Project is an initiative of public libraries together with local museums and archives with the aim of digitising material from their local studies collections.

Thom's directories for the following years have been indexed on Ask About Ireland and a search will bring up a scan of the original page:

- 1862, 1887–89, 1892, 1912, 1921, 1925–28, 1930–32, 1934–36, 1940–41, 1943, 1965, 1971–80, 1985–86.

The directories may be found at **http://bit.ly/3GMGIbY**.

Trade Directory, 1931
This directory covers towns in the Republic of Ireland. Transcriptions are available on Findmypast and Ancestry with a subscription. It is also freely available at **www.from-ireland.net/trade-directory**.

Maps of Dublin accompanying Thom's Official Directory
University College Dublin has digitised nine maps that were originally published in *Thom's Almanac and Official Directory*. The dates of the maps available are between 1874 and 1898 and they are free to view at **http://bit.ly/3koKlwW**.

Chapter 8

GAZETTEERS AND TOPOGRAPHICAL DICTIONARIES

The definition of a gazetteer is a geographical list or dictionary of place names that come in three types, alphabetical list, dictionary and encyclopaedic. A topographical dictionary is a description of places arranged alphabetically.

These dry descriptions really do not do justice to the huge amount of information contained in these works. Not only do they describe the landscape your ancestors lived in but they include information about the history of the area, the industries, population statistics, the landowners, the manor courts and very usefully, historic or alternative names of places. This is particularly helpful if you are searching within older records for a place that has used a different name in the past.

The key texts from the late eighteenth and the nineteenth century that specifically cover Ireland are included here.

Seward's Hibernian Gazetteer, 1789

According to *DIB*, William Wenman Seward was an attorney and writer who conducted his legal practice in Dublin and died there in 1805. He published his *Hibernian Gazetteer* in 1789 which was well received by the public and later followed it up with an expanded *Topographia Hibernica* in 1797.

Check with WorldCat for your nearest hard copy version of this book or you may be able to access an online version through a university library membership.

Seward's Topographia Hibernica, 1797

This work by William Wenman Seward was produced a year before the United Irishmen's Rebellion of 1798 while Ireland was still a separate kingdom and before the Act of Union 1800. The information contained in this book includes:

> Antiquities, natural curiosities, trade, manufactures, extent and population. Its counties, baronies, cities, borough, parliamentary representation and patronage, ancient districts and their original proprietors. Post, market and fair towns. Bishoprics, ecclesiastical benefices, abbeys, monasteries, castles, ruins, private seats and remarkable buildings. Mountains, rivers, lakes, mineral-springs, bays and harbours, with the latitude and longitude of the principal places and their distances from the metropolis and from each other. Historical anecdotes and remarkable events.

The 338-page book provides little by way of names other than the large landowners and some historical figures. However, it is clear that Hansbrow used much of the material as a source for his 1835 *Hibernian Gazetteer* (see below).

Topographia Hibernica has a number of very good illustrations, such as that of Carlow Castle. This book is freely available at the Wellcome Collection: **http://bit.ly/3GSdtVc** and at Hathi Trust: **http://bit.ly/3kuq6hH**.

Description of Wicklow town, County Wicklow in Seward's Topographia Hibernica. (Courtesy the Wellcome Collection)

> WICKLOW *town*, fit. in bar. Newcaſtle, co. Wicklow, prov. Leinſter, 24 miles from Dublin: it is a market, poſt and fair town, and the ſhire and aſſizes town for that co. It is ſeated on the ſea ſide, and has a narrow haven at the mouth of the river *Leitrim*, fit only for ſmall veſſels which carry proviſions to the capital, and that indeed is its chief trade; here is a rock, by ſome taken for the remains of a caſtle, ſurrounded by a ſtrong wall. There are but few buildings, yet it has a barrack, and is remarkable for the beſt *ale* in the kingdom: about a mile and an half on the E. is a point of land called *Wicklow-head*. This place is a vicarage in dioc. of Dublin, and gives title of viſc. to the family of *Howard*, and was antiently called *Wykenlooe*. Fairs held 28 Mar. Aſcenſion-day, 12 Aug. and 25 Nov. Wicklow returns 2 members to parliament, patronage in the *Tighe* family. Lat. 52 : 7, lon. 6 : 30.

Engraving of Carlow Castle from Topographia Hibernica, 1797. (Courtesy of the Wellcome Collection)

Carlisle's Topographical Dictionary of Ireland, 1810

A Topographical Dictionary of Ireland was written by Nicholas Carlisle (1771–1847), a Fellow of the Society of Antiquaries of London and published in 1810.

Carlisle had previously written the two-volume *Topographical Dictionary of England* (1808) and subsequently produced the *Topographical Dictionary of Wales* (1811) and the *Topographical Dictionary of Scotland* (1813).

The Irish volume, which ran to 742 pages, included:

> the names of the several cities, towns, parishes and villages, with the barony, county and province to which they respectively belong. The valuation and present state of the ecclesiastical benefices. The distance and bearing of every place from the nearest post office and of the post offices from the metropolis. Fairs. Members of Parliament and corporations. Charter schools and assizes to which is added miscellaneous information respecting the monastic foundations and other matters of local history. Collected from the most authentic documents and arranged in alphabetical order.

The preface demonstrated a particular interest in the state of the Established Church (the Church of Ireland) in each diocese and the returns completed by Church of Ireland clergy in 1805 and 1806 provide the basis of much of the information in this work. There are few names other than the names of the Church of Ireland clergy to be found within this volume.

Carlisle included a list of the most important historical and topographical books he had consulted in the compilation of his work.

Carlisle's *Topographical Dictionary of Ireland* is freely available at Internet Archive: **http://bit.ly/3QRUoH1**.

Carlisle's entry for the town of Wicklow, County Wicklow is shown below.

> WICKLOW, in the Barony of Newcastle, Co. of WICKLOW, and Province of Leinster: a V., with the Prebend in St. Patrick's Cathedral annexed; and Episcopally united, time immemorial, to the R. and V. of Drumkey, and the V. of Kelpole, together with the Chapels of Glanely, Kilcommon, Killesky, Killoughter, and Rathnew: the Prebend of Wicklow is valued in the King's Books at £10. *Irish* Money, and the V. at £3..6..8: a Church, in good order, at Wicklow; and a Chapel, in good order, at Glanely: no Glebe House: a Glebe, of 32 a. 2 r. 22 p., at Drumkey, near the church; another, of 4 acres, one mile from the church; and a third, of 3 a. 3 r. 27 p., near Glanely: The Rev. Robert Baylis Dealtry, LL. D., the Incumbent (in 1806), who has cure of souls, and a Stall in the Cathedral: the duties are performed by two Resident Curates, viz., The Rev. Robert Porter, of Wicklow, at a Salary of £75. *per annum*, and also from the County, for attending the Gaol, £30.: The Rev. James Corcoran, of Glanely, at a Salary of £100. *per annum.* Wicklow is in the Dioceses of Dublin and Glandelagh, and Province of Dublin. It is 24 m. S. S. E. from Dublin. The Fairs are holden on the 28th of March, Ascension-day, 12th of August, and 25th of November. It is situate on the Irish Sea. It has six Post-days in the week. It is the Shire Town, and where the Assizes are holden; and gives title of Viscount to the family of Howard. The Magistrates are a Portrieve, and Recorder.

The description of Wicklow town, County Wicklow in Carlisle's Topographical Dictionary of Ireland. (Courtesy of Internet Archive)

Hansbrow's Hibernian Gazetteer, 1835

An Improved Topographical and Historical Hibernian Gazetteer to which is added An Introduction to the Ancient and Modern History of Ireland by Reverend G. Hansbrow was published in 1835.

The publication includes a description of the various boroughs, baronies, buildings, cities, counties, collieries, castles, church, curiosities, fisheries, glens, harbours, lakes, mines, mountains, provinces, parishes, rivers, spas, seats, towers, towns, villages, waterfalls, etc.

George Hansbrow (1774–1864) was a Wesleyan minister who lived in Kilkenny and in Dublin and who had been collecting material for his book during intervals in his ministerial work. He believed that there was a deficiency of such works due to the time, difficulty and expense required to produce them.

Although the language is quite flowery, this work is interesting for its occasionally waspish observations. Hansbrow wrote:

> During the prosecution of this work the Compiler was often led to believe, if our ungrateful and tasteless absentee gentry had only read the topography of their own country, much of the time and money they have spent in foreign lands, would have been more usefully spent at home; and they would also have found, on trial, few parts of the world more deserving of notice than poor, deserted, ill-fated Ireland.

His observations on Wicklow town are shown below and it is interesting to compare Hansbrow's entry with Carlisle's for the same town shown above:

> Wicklow Town situated in the county Wicklow, province of Leinster, 24 miles from Dublin. It is a market, post and fair town, and the shire and assizes town for that county. It is seated on the sea-side and has a narrow haven at the mouth of the river Leitrim, fit only for small vessels, which carry provisions to the capital and that indeed is its chief trade. Here is a rock by some taken for the remains of a castle, surrounded by a strong wall; and is remarkable for the best ale in the kingdom. In addition to the old church there are also chapels for the Calvinists, Romanists, Methodists, and Quakers. There are two Romish free schools, but for want of funds and patriotism the old Protestant free school is extinct. There is a barrack, courthouse, gaol and dispensary. The Ballast-Office of Dublin offered to make a good harbour here, if the Wicklow corporation would give them up their harbour's duties, who, unfortunately, were then so penny wise and pound foolish, refused, to the great injury of the town and vicinity. The new road from Arklow will bring those towns by travelling five miles nearer, beside evading the mountains. This town gives title of earl to the noble family of Howard. Fair days, March 28, Ascension-day August 12 and November 25. Market, Saturday. Population 2,472.

The Hibernian Gazetteer is freely available on Google Books: **http://bit.ly/3CT7ka8** and at Internet Archive: **http://bit.ly/3XjApDP**.

Lewis's Topographical Dictionary of Ireland, 1837

Often seen as the pre-eminent topographical dictionary of Ireland, Lewis's work was first published in 1837 in two volumes. Volume 1 covers A to J and Volume 2 covers K to Y, there being no place names beginning with Z. Volume 2 also has an index of place names for both volumes.

Samuel Lewis (1782–1865) also published *A Topographical Dictionary of England* in seven editions between 1831 and 1849, *A Topographical Dictionary of Wales* in five editions between 1833 and 1850 and *A Topographical Dictionary of Scotland* in two editions between 1846 and 1851.

In the introduction to the first volume, Lewis noted that there was ample information available to use in the compilation of the volumes for England and Wales. The lack of such information for Ireland, however, required greater personal survey which increased the expense.

Lewis's aim was to give in a condensed form, a faithful and impartial description of each place. To achieve that, he sought information from local gentlemen who later checked proof sheets and made any necessary amendments. Statistics for population and number of houses were extracted from the 1831 census and the Ordnance Survey, which was still progressing with its first mapping of Ireland, was consulted with regard to number of acres in parishes.

Arms and seals of cities, boroughs, corporate towns, bishoprics, etc. were engraved from drawings made from impressions in wax and the greatest care was taken to reproduce an exact facsimile of the original.

In contrast with the information provided by earlier authors about the town of Wicklow, Lewis's entry runs to two full pages and he provides more information about the castle alluded to in earlier accounts:

> Its ancient name Wykinglo or Wykinglogh is derived from its situation at the southern extremity of a creek shut out from the sea by a long narrow peninsula called the Murragh. It is supposed to have been one of the maritime stations occupied by the Danes previously to the landing of the English in 1169, and to have been called by them Wigginge Lough, 'the Lake of Ships'.
>
> Afterwards it formed part of the extensive possessions granted by Strongbow to Maurice Fitzgerald who commenced the building of a castle here for the protection of his property, the execution of which was discontinued in consequence of his death in 1176. His sons were subsequently dispossessed of their inheritance by William Fitz-Aldelm and compelled to accept in exchange for it the decayed and defenceless city of Ferns.

In 1301 the town was burned by the Irish; but the castle was put into a state of defence in 1375 by William Fitzwilliam, a descendant of one of the early English settlers, in whose family the constableship continued for several generations.

From its vicinity to the Irish mountain septs it was a frequent subject of contention. In the early part of the sixteenth century it fell into the hands of the Byrnes, the chieftains of the northern part of the county, by whom the castle and town were surrendered to Henry VIII in 1543.

In 1641, Luke O'Toole invested the castle, but was forced to raise the siege on the approach of Sir Charles Coote, who sullied his victory by an unauthorised and indiscriminate slaughter of the inhabitants of the town.

From these first few paragraphs, we have much more detailed historical information and family names than that provided in earlier works.

The first volume may be freely accessed at Google Books: **http://bit.ly/3D23CL8** and the second volume is freely available at Internet Archive: **http://bit.ly/3iQeapX**.

Volumes 1 and 2 are also available at My Heritage and at Ancestry with a subscription.

A second edition of the *Topographical Dictionary of Ireland* was published in 1849. Volume 1 **http://bit.ly/3GVFGKv** and Volume 2 **http://bit.ly/3HhcizM** are both freely available at Google Books.

The common seal of Wicklow Borough in Lewis's Topographical Dictionary of Ireland, 1837, Volume 2. (Courtesy of Internet Archive)

Lewis's Atlas to the Topographical Dictionary of Ireland, 1846

A companion *Atlas to the Topographical Dictionary of Ireland* was published in 1846 and featured maps of each county showing the barony divisions.

The map of County Meath is reproduced here. *The Atlas* may be freely accessed on Google Books: **http://bit.ly/3krfNuE**.

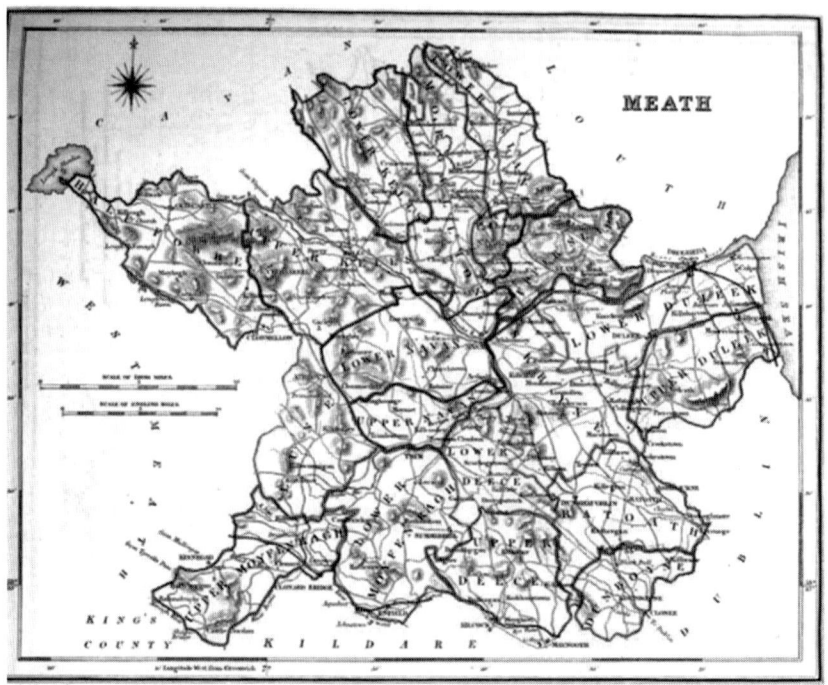

Map of County Meath from Lewis's Atlas of Ireland. (Courtesy of Google Books)

Ordnance Survey Memoirs, 1830s

While the *Ordnance Survey Memoirs* are not in the traditional mould of topographical dictionaries or gazetteers, they are important for the information they provide on Irish culture and society in the pre-famine era.

In 1824, the prime minister, the Duke of Wellington, authorised the first Ordnance Survey of Ireland with maps to the scale of 6 inches to 1 statute mile. The survey was directed by Colonel Thomas Colby who commanded officers of the Royal Engineers and three companies of sappers and miners. Civil assistants were recruited to help with the sketching, drawing and engraving of maps and, eventually, in the 1830s, the writing of the *Memoirs*.

Reports were written by officers and civil assistants under supervision who were provided with Heads of Inquiry under which information was to be reported.

Between 1839 and 1840 the *Memoirs* scheme collapsed as the government could no longer countenance the ongoing expenditure. Consequently, the scheme was discontinued before the southern half of Ireland was covered.

Only one *Memoir* was published at the time – the parish of Templemore, County Londonderry; the remaining manuscripts were moved to storage in the RIA, Dublin.

In the 1990s, the Institute of Irish Studies at Queen's University, Belfast published the memoirs in forty volumes covering the northern counties of Ireland. The volumes are laid out on a parish basis although there is one glaring omission as there is no memoir for Belfast.

There is also a very comprehensive separately published index that includes lists of drawings, maps, parishes, volumes and memoir writers.

Described by the UHF as a nineteenth-century Domesday Book, the *Memoirs* describe the landscape, buildings, antiquities, land holdings, population, employment, livelihood, housing and medical care. They provide the names of the landlords, the schools and schoolmasters, the religious establishments as well as the entertainment, beliefs, customs and superstitions of the locals.

The *Memoirs* often have the personal opinion of those who compiled them and they are not always complimentary.

James Boyle who wrote the *Memoir* for my hometown of Ballymena, in the parish of Kirkinriola, County Antrim, was fairly scathing about the inhabitants. Volume 23, County Antrim has the following entry by Boyle:

> The Ballymena people are but little disposed for amusement, there being no public amusement nor convivial meetings. In the town there is little society except among families which are connected or intermarried … the people being chiefly engaged in business and solely bent upon making money … The Ballymena people are neither polished nor aristocratic in their manners, nor do they possess any taste. They are rather a moral race (though the number of public houses, there being 107, would lead one to suppose otherwise). They are indeed rather fond of whiskey and too many indulge in it.

Many of the Antrim and Londonderry parishes include information about emigration with names, ages and religion of the emigrants along with the townland they lived in and the port to which they went.

For example, the parish of Artrea in County Londonderry, has a list of the names of inhabitants who emigrated in 1834 and 1835. One family that emigrated in 1834 was:

- Henery Hillman, Roman Catholic, aged 30 from Aughrim to New York
- Hercules Hillman, Roman Catholic, aged 17 from Aughrim to New York
- Cathrine Hillman, Roman Catholic, aged 45 from Aughrim to New York
- Elenor Hillman, Roman Catholic, aged 20 from Aughrim to New York

Names have been reproduced as found in the *Memoir*. This record of the Hillman family emigrating to New York may be the only one that connects them to a specific place in Ireland.

The volumes by county are as follows:

- Antrim – 2, 8, 10, 13, 16, 19, 21, 23, 24, 26, 29, 32, 35, 37
- Armagh – 1
- Donegal – 38, 39
- Down – 3, 7, 12, 17
- Fermanagh – 4, 14
- Londonderry – 6, 9, 11, 15, 18, 22, 25, 27, 28, 30, 31, 33, 34, 36
- Tyrone – 5, 20
- South Ulster – Volume 40 includes some parishes in counties Cavan, Leitrim, Louth, Monaghan and Sligo

The *Ordnance Survey Memoirs* may be purchased from Books Ireland www.booksireland.org.uk and they are available in many libraries.

Parliamentary Gazetteer of Ireland, 1846

The *Parliamentary Gazetteer of Ireland* was published in three volumes in 1846.

The front page noted that it was 'adapted to the new poor-law, franchise, municipal and ecclesiastical arrangements and compiled with a specific reference to the lines of railroad and canal communication as existing in 1844–45.'

Illustrated by a series of maps and other plates, it presented the results, in detail, of the census of 1841, compared with that of 1831.

The Poor Law had been introduced to Ireland in 1838 in response to widespread poverty. Initially, 130 Poor Law Unions were set up, based in market towns, each of which had a workhouse to provide relief for the destitute.

The Great Famine of Ireland caused by potato blight started in 1845 and so the publication of the *Parliamentary Gazetteer* coincided with it.

Drawing on the reports of commissioners and inspectors, the *Gazetteer* provided an introduction that included a summary and statistics on subjects such as crime figures, agricultural production, prisons, lunatic asylums, the constabulary, military, parliamentary representation, education, literature, religion, poor laws, loan funds, wages, emigration, house accommodation, population and livestock. Regarding lunatic asylums, the inspector-generals wrote:

> The places of confinement, public and private, are placed by act of parliament under the commissioner's inspection. The only public asylums that existed when they commenced duty in 1821 for the cure of this malady, were those of Dublin and Cork, exclusive of a few private asylums, chiefly in the neighbourhood of Dublin, which were conducted on humane and judicious principles; all others were temporary receptacles for idiots and incurable cases, in the gaols and house of industry scattered through the county towns, and where no means could be provided for the cure and proper care of such patients. Classification and healthy employment could not be obtained in such places, and their cases appeared hopeless. At the commissioner's suggestion, in the year 1823, an act of parliament passed, legalizing district lunatic asylums, at the joint expense of three or more counties. In the following year three of them were in progress of building, viz at Armagh, Limerick and Belfast … there now exist nine of them. Thus is established a national school for discovering the best mode of treating this disease, a ground-work is laid for a house of reception for all pauper cases of lunacy or idiotism in the kingdom, only requiring an additional wing to the building as numbers increase.

Mental illness was poorly understood in these times and there seemed to be little distinction between it and what we refer to now as learning difficulties. Pity the people admitted to such institutions who could not afford to pay for private care.

The *Gazetteer* continues with detailed information on counties, parishes, islands, towns and villages that contained at least twenty houses and the volumes are laid out alphabetically by place name.

Volume 1 covers place names A to C and is freely available at Internet Archive: **http://bit.ly/3Hjnps7**.

Volume 2 covers place names D to M and is freely available on Google Books: **http://bit.ly/3XJoyi5**.

Volume 3 covers place names O to Y and also has an index. It is freely available at Internet Archive: **http://bit.ly/3Hg7B9B**.

Chapter 9

ONLINE LIBRARIES AND PORTALS

There are a number of online libraries that provide free, online access to out-of-copyright material on a myriad of subjects. These are of tremendous value to the genealogist and allow the researcher to assemble a virtual library at no cost and without having to find shelf space.

You will find books and journals containing transcripts of parish registers, travel books, histories, passenger lists, headstone inscriptions, church histories and family genealogies.

It is a useful exercise to do a search on each of these sites to check what might be available for the names in your family tree or for their townland, village, town, parish or county of origin.

Do be aware that while there are a large number of family genealogies available, the quality of them varies considerably. As with any ancestral research, check that each fact presented is backed up with a reference or a source and if at all possible, replicate that search and find the original document to reassure yourself that it is accurate and what it claims to be.

This chapter covers the main online libraries, many of which have free access. Portals with links to books are also provided.

Internet Archive
https://archive.org
The Internet Archive first began in 1996 by archiving websites and moved on to providing digital versions of other published works. The free-to-access collection is growing on a daily basis; at the time of writing the archive held:

- 735 billion web pages
- 41 million books and texts

- 14.7 million audio recordings (including 240,000 live concerts)
- 8.4 million videos (including 2.4 million television news programmes)
- 4.4 million images
- 890,000 software programs

Through the Open Library, modern books that are still within copyright may be borrowed for one hour at a time – just register for a free account.

One of the available historical books about Belfast is Young, Robert M. (ed.) *Historical Notices of Old Belfast and its Vicinity*, Belfast, 1896. Chapters in this work include:

- Assizes held in Ulster, 1615
- Description of the Ardes Barony, 1683
- Diary of Colonel Bellingham at Belfast, 1690
- Depositions of the Island Magee Witches, 1710
- Life of Mary Ann McCracken, 1770–1866
- The Scheme to Transplant the Scots from Ulster, 1653

Names of individuals are provided, such as those who were tried at the Assizes of 1615. One of those who appeared before the Grand Jury in

Irish Peasant Girl Spinning from Young's *Historical Notices of Belfast and its Vicinity*, 1896. (Courtesy of Internet Archive)

Carrickfergus, County Antrim on 12 March 1615 was Brian O'Gribben of Edendufcarricke (now Randalstown), a yeoman who on the 27 November 1614 committed an assault upon Elise ny Lagan, the widow of William Toole, a faithful subject:

> [A]nd with 'a cudgill' worth one halfpenny which he had in his right hand, he struck her in the front of the head, giving her a mortal wound of four inches in length and one inch deep, of which she languished until the last day of the same month, when she died. Guilty. Says he is a Clerk. He is therefore, as is shewn in a former case, branded in the left hand and delivered to the Ordinary.

The book is interspersed throughout with lists of names and with images such as that of the Irish peasant girl spinning.

Some other books found at Internet Archive that provide historical information about Belfast are:

- Joy, Henry, *Historical Collections Relative to the Town of Belfast from the Earliest Period to the Union with Great Britain*, Belfast, 1817.
- Benn, George, *A History of the Town of Belfast from the Earliest Times to the Close of the Eighteenth Century*, London, 1877. Includes pen pictures of prominent Belfast families such as Le Squire, Walcot, Leathes, Theaker, Haddock, Doak, Martin, Waring, Macartney, Pottinger, Knox, Legge and Eccles.
- Benn, George, *A History of the Town of Belfast With an Accurate Account of Its Former and Present State With a Statistical Survey of the Parish of Belfast*, Belfast, 1877.
- Young, Robert M. (ed), *The Town Book of the Corporation of Belfast 1613–1816*, Belfast, 1892. Includes lists of names such as burgesses, freemen, militia and so on connected with Belfast.

Google Books
https://books.google.com

Perform a search on Google Books and you will be provided with a number of results, some of which have no information other than the title, author and publishing information, some for which a snippet of information about the search term is provided and some which allow a free preview or a percentage of the book.

Some books that have been digitised are available to buy through Google Books and can be downloaded to your Google Play library.

However, there are also a large number of out-of-copyright books that can be accessed for free and saved to your virtual library shelves on Google Play.

Some such as Burke's *A Genealogical and Heraldic Dictionary of Landed Gentry of Ireland,* London, 1858 provide copious information on the ancestry of families throughout Ireland.

Others such as the 'Select Committee on Fictitious Votes (1837)', *Third Report from the Select Committees on Fictitious Votes, Ireland, Vol 11, Part 2,* House of Commons, 1837 provides the names of voters in towns and cities throughout Ireland, names of spirit sellers and members of guilds.

Hathi Trust
www.hathitrust.org
The Hathi Trust is a partnership of academic and research institutions, offering a collection of titles digitised from libraries around the world. It has millions of books freely available and also references the libraries where books may be found if they are not digitised. There is a useful variety of genealogy books, family histories, etc., many of which have an Irish focus.

Register for a free guest account and you have the option of saving books to your collections, which can be made private or public.

Those who have Scots-Irish / Ulster-Scots ancestry will be particularly interested in Black, George Fraser, *The Surnames of Scotland, Their Origin, Meaning and History,* New York, 1962. This work is still considered a key text for researching Scottish ancestor's surnames.

Family Search Digital Library
www.familysearch.org/library/books
Another valuable addition to the online library offerings is the Family Search Digital Library, which describes itself as 'the largest genealogical library in the world'.

It is actively digitising family histories, local histories and other collections to make them searchable and freely available to researchers worldwide.

It has partnered with institutions and organisations such as: Allen County Public Library Genealogy Center; Arizona State Library; Birmingham Public Library; Brigham Young Family History Library; Columbus Metropolitan Library; Houston Public Library; Dallas Public Library; George A. Smathers Libraries at the University of Florida; Historical Society of Pennsylvania; Midwest Genealogy Center; Onondaga County Public Library; Ontario Ancestors; St Louis County Library; Miriam Weiner Routes to Roots Collection; Southern California Genealogical Society and Library and Provo Daughters of Utah Pioneers Museum.

There are different access levels and not all of the results in a search are publicly available due to copyright restrictions. Nevertheless, there are still thousands of books and journals available – try doing a search on your family name or the location they lived in. Publicly available publications may be downloaded to your computer.

For example, a search for County Kildare provides 233,238 publicly available results such as:

- *The Journal of the County Kildare Archaeological Society*
- Marquis of Kildare, *The earls of Kildare and their ancestors from 1057 to 1773 by the Marquis of Kildare,* Dublin, 1864
- Prime, Temple, *Some account of the Palmer family of Rahan, County Kildare, Ireland,* New York, 1903
- Landed Estates Court, *The Estate of Walter Fitzgerald, County Kildare, Ireland,* Dublin, 1868
- Jones, Robert, L., *Mylod genealogy; the descendants of Patrick Mylod and Mary McAvoy of counties Offaly and Kildare,* Ireland, 1982

You will need to register for a free account before accessing the Family Search Digital Library.

Project Gutenberg
www.gutenberg.org

Project Gutenberg was founded in 1971 and offers over 60,000 free e-books available to download as well as a range of periodicals, most of which are out-of-copyright materials. You can choose among free e-pub and Kindle e-books, download them or read them online.

Unlike other digital libraries mentioned here, the focus in Project Gutenberg is not on genealogy, but there are still publications that you may find of interest such as:

- Falls, Cyril, *The History of the 36th (Ulster) Division,* London, 1922
- O'Rourke, Rev. John, *The History of the Great Irish Famine of 1847 with Notices of Earlier Irish Famines,* Dublin, 1902

Genealogy Gophers
www.gengophers.com

This is a very useful site that enables you to search over 80,000 genealogy books – searching can be by name, location, date range, relatives' names or title of a publication – this site is well worth a visit.

The search results will provide links to the digital item. Viewing up to three books a week is free, but they ask for a small donation to view more results.

Free Irish E-books Index
http://freeirishgenebooks.blogspot.com

This site provides an index and link to over 4,000 free e-books and journals on the topics of Irish history, biography and genealogy, most of which can be downloaded for free.

Categories include:

- Pedigrees listed alphabetically
- Family Histories listed alphabetically
- Diaspora
- Resources that include almanacs, directories, church records, guide books, journals, nobility and landed gentry, holdings of Irish family and estate papers, Irish genealogy resources

A click on any of these categories opens up a long list of links to genealogy resources such as the listings under the D section of family and estate papers.

D
- DALTON: Papers of Alfred Dalton - b. Cork 1892 - African railways - Photograph - BOD
- DARLEY: Sir Frederick Matthew Darley - b. Dublin, 1830, Chief Justice of NSW Supreme Court - NSWML - **Frederick Matthew Darly** in Wikipedia
- DAWSON: Dartrey Papers - Dawson family of Dawson Grove, alias Dartrey, Co. Monaghan; also Cos. Armagh, Louth, Waterford, Tipperary, Fermanagh etc. - PRONI
- De BURCA/BURKE: Papers of Seamus de Burca (James Bourke): playwright - NLI
- De VERE: See HUNT, De VERE - LCC
- De VESCI/VESEY, MUSCHAMP, BOYLE, LANE: De Vesci Papers (89) - Viscounts de Vesci and related families of Muschamp, Boyle/Blessington, Lane/ Lanesborough; estates in Queen's Co, Cork City and County; Co. Down, Dublin City and County, Counties Carlow, Galway, Kildare, Kilkenny, King's County, Limerick City and County, Counties Mayo, Roscommon, Waterford City and County, Co. Wexford (and in England: Devon, Dorset, Hampshire, Kent, Wiltshire) - NLI
- D'ARCY, PALIN, DOPPING, SIRR, WAKEFIELD, LEWIS: D'Arcy of Hyde Park Papers (134) - Co. Westmeath; small no. of papers of related families Palin, Dopping, Sirr, Wakefield, Lewis - NLI
- DILLON: Clonbrock Estate Papers (54) - family of Dillon, Barons Clonbrock, Ahascragh, Co. Galway - NLI
- DILLON: Papers of Geraldine Plunkett Dillon (43) - NLI
- DONOUGHMORE: For the Earl of Donoughmore see HELY-HUTCHINSON - eBook
- DOPPING: See D'ARCY, PALIN, DOPPING, SIRR, WAKEFIELD, LEWIS - NLI
- DOPPING-HEPENSTAL: Dopping-Hepenstal Papers (61) - of Derrycassen, Co. Longford - NLI
- DOWDEN: Alderman Richard Dowden (b1794-d1861), Mayor of Cork in 1845, businessman, liberal, philanthropist. U140 List - CCCA
- DOYNE: Doyne Papers (24) - family formerly of Wells, Gorey, County Wexford - NLI
- DUKE: Papers of Henry Duke - Chief Secretary for Ireland 1916 - 1918 - BOD
- DUNLAP, RUTHERFORD: Dunlap/Delap Papers - **Dunlap, Rutherford** families of Strabane, Co. Tyrone; John Dunlap of Philadelphia; **Delap** of Ramelton and Ray, Co. Donegal - PRONI

Listings under D of Family and Estate Papers at the Index of Free Irish E-books. (Courtesy of Peter J. Clarke)

Northern Ireland Libraries
www.librariesni.org.uk

With Northern Ireland Libraries you can access e-books, audiobooks, magazines and newspapers for free. There are over 17,000 e-books and over 160 e-magazines to choose from. You can join online for free and the only stipulation is that you must live, work or study in Northern Ireland. Once you have your library card, you can access the publications through the Libby, Pressreader and Borrowbox apps.

Libraries Ireland
www.librariesireland.ie/elibrary

Within the Republic of Ireland, Libraries Ireland provides access to e-books, e-audiobooks, e-magazines, e-learning courses and online newspapers. Membership of Libraries Ireland is freely available to residents. Apply for your library card and then access the publications through the Libby, Pressreader and Borrowbox apps.

Ask About Ireland
www.askaboutireland.ie/reading-room/digital-book-collection

The Ask About Ireland website provides free access to a number of e-books that have been donated by libraries in Ireland. These can be searched by keyword or browsed by place or subject and there are also talking e-books. For example, a search of publications for County Galway includes:

- D'Alton, Right Rev., *History of the Archdiocese of Tuam, Volumes 1 and 2*, Dublin, 1928
- Dutton, Hely, *A Statistical and Agricultural Survey of the County of Galway*, Dublin, 1824
- Hardiman, James, *The History of the Town and County of the Town of Galway*, Dublin, 1820

Subscription Websites

The three main subscription websites have digitised books in their collections. However, be aware that most of the books they hold will be freely available in other collections such as Internet Archive, Open Library, Hathi Trust, Google Books or your local library.

The armorial ensigns of the fourteen ancient families of Galway. From Hardiman, James, The History of the Town and County of the Town of Galway, Dublin, 1820. (Courtesy of the LGMA)

Findmypast
www.findmypast.co.uk
Findmypast has digitised a number of books, some of which are indexed and fully searchable and others that can be browsed but are not indexed.

In addition to the Street Directories and Almanacs addressed in Chapter Seven some of the books available on the website are:

- O'Hart's *The Irish Landed Gentry When Cromwell Came to Ireland*, 1887
- Armagh Registers and Records that comprises one publication, i.e., *Historical Memoirs of the City of Armagh*, 1819
- Wicklow Registers and Records that comprises *Corn Growers, Carriers & Traders, County Wicklow, 1788, 1789 & 1790; Kilcoole School Registers, 1862; Newcastle School Registers, 1864–1948; Shillielagh & Ballinacor South Memorial, 1837*; and *The People of Wicklow, 1798; The Rebellion*
- Church of Ireland Histories and Reference Guides that comprises *The National Churches: The Church of Ireland*, 1892 and *Some Worthies of the Irish Church*, 1900
- Kerry Histories and Reference Guides which comprises *A History of the Kingdom of Kerry*, 1871; *A Pictorial and Descriptive Guide to Killarney, The Kerry coast, Glengariff, Cork and the South West of Ireland*, 1880; and *The Ancient and Present State of the County of Kerry*, 1756

Ancestry
www.ancestry.com
Ancestry has digitised a number of books, many of which are indexed and searchable and it is also possible to browse the publications. Some of the books of available are:

- Ireland, Casey Collection Indexes, 1545–1960
  This collection contains an index and images from a series of books titled, *O'Kief, Coshe Mang, Slieve Lougher and the Upper Blackwater in Ireland* by Albert E. Casey. There were sixteen volumes in the Casey Collection, a compilation of genealogical and historical records from counties Cork and Kerry, Ireland.
- *Later Scots-Irish Links, 1725–1825*
  David Dobson's publication covers Scots living in Ulster and Irish living in Scotland over a 100-year period and has around 1,200 names.
- History of O'Mullally and Lally clan
  This book by Dennis Patrick O'Mullally was published in 1941 with the full title of *History of O'Mullally and Lally Clann or The history of an Irish Family through the Ages enterwined with that of the Irish Nation*.

- *Jacobites of Lowland Scotland, England, Ireland, France and Spain*, 1745
  Published in 2002, Frances McDonnell's work records 1,500 followers of the House of Stuart who attempted to regain the throne of Great Britain from the ruling House of Hanover and who took part in the Jacobite rebellions.

My Heritage
www.myheritage.com

A number of books and reference works that relate to Ireland are to be found here such as:

- *Dod's Peerage, Baronetage, Knightage, etc. of Great Britain and Ireland for 1920*, London, 1919
- *Irish Tourist: in a Series of Picturesque Views, Travelling Incidents, and Observations, Statistical, Political and Moral on the Character and Aspect of the Irish Nation*, Dublin, 1815
- *The United Irishmen, Their Lives and Times*, Dublin, 1803

The Digital Repository of Ireland
https://dri.ie

The Digital Repository of Ireland (DRI) launched to the public in 2015 and it provides free access to social and cultural digital data in the fields of arts, social sciences and humanities, and partners with a range of organisations. A sample of some of the collections that may be of particular interest to family historians researching their Irish ancestors are:

- The Royal Dublin Fusiliers Association (RDFA) Archive
  The RDFA was established in 1996 to commemorate all Irish men and women who volunteered, served and died in the First World War, 1914–1918. In 2005, the Association placed its archive with Dublin City Library and Archive, some of which is now available to view on DRI.
- Congregation of the Sisters of Mercy
  Register of students admitted to Our Lady of Mercy Training College, Baggot Street and Carysfort Teacher Training College, Dublin between 1883 and 1922. Biographical information is provided on the trainee teachers such as names, address, age, marital status, where born, when appointed as a teacher, etc.
- Dublin City Library and Archive
  There are a number of interesting collections in this archive including Dublin City Council Manuscript Minutes, 1841–1881; Fáilte Ireland

Tourism Photographic Collection; Jacob's Biscuit Factory Archive and Dublin City Electoral Lists.
- Fingal Local Studies and Archives
Fingal and the Fight for Irish Freedom photographic collection has memorabilia connected to Fingallians involved in the revolutionary period (1912–1923).
- Irish Capuchin Provincial Archives
The Capuchins and the Irish Revolution contains correspondence and papers of Capuchin priests detailing their involvement with participants in the national struggle. The majority of the material dates from 1916 to 1925 and includes many records highlighting the role played by Irish Capuchins in ministering to Republican leaders and their relations.
- National Archives of Ireland
There are three collections – Documents of Irish Foreign Policy; The Inspiring Ireland Project and Records of Dáil Éireann.

Northern Ireland Community Archive
https://niarchive.org/
The Northern Ireland Community Archive is a collection of tourist trails, museum collections, photographs, exhibitions, oral testimonies and other information from local museums and community groups.

Although the bulk of items seem to originate in the Causeway Coast and Glens of Antrim, there are items of interest for the genealogist, some of which are:

- Moyle Migrations; Exploring Family Histories from Rathlin, Ballycastle and the Glens
- Ballymoney (County Antrim) Old Church Graveyard, an Illustrated Guide
- NI100: 100 Years Famous Sons and Daughters of the Causeway Coast and Glens
- The Parish of Derrykeighan; A Rammel Through North Antrim, The Who, The What, The Where
- Place names and Fieldnames of Culfeightrin (County Antrim)

Chapter 10

BOOK PUBLISHERS

Although books on Irish history, culture, biography, folklore and customs are available from many publishers and sellers, this chapter focuses on those publishers who offer books of interest specifically for the genealogist researching Irish family history. These books are often available from diverse booksellers in hard copy and e-book formats.

Blackstaff Press
https://blackstaffpress.com
Based in Belfast, Blackstaff Press publishes titles from a range of genres and sells local interest books. Some of interest to the genealogist are:

- Breen, Colin, *A Force Like No Other*, Books 1, 2 and 3, 2017–2021
- Hartley, Tom, *Balmoral Cemetery: The History of Belfast, Written in Stone, Book 3*, 2019
- Orr, Philip, *The Road to the Somme*, 2018

Books Ireland
www.booksireland.org.uk
Books Ireland is the publishing arm of the Ulster Historical Foundation, a commercial research company. It sells books such as the *Ordnance Survey Memoirs* and also publishes a range of its own work such as:

- Dickson, R.J., *Ulster Emigration to Colonial America, 1718–1775*, Belfast, 2016
- Robinson, Philip S., *The Plantation of Ulster: British Settlement in an Irish Landscape, 1600–1670*, Belfast, 2000
- Roulston, William, *Researching Presbyterian Ancestors in Ireland*, Belfast, 2020

Flyleaf Press
www.ancestornetwork.ie/shop
Flyleaf Press is the publishing arm of Ancestor Network, a commercial research company. Most of its publications are guides for tracing your ancestors in particular counties such as Westmeath, Tipperary and Leitrim, although there are a few others such as Ryan, James G., *Sources for Irish Family History: A Listing of Books and Articles on The History of Irish Families*, Dublin, 2021.

Four Courts Press
www.fourcourtspress.ie/welcome
An academic book publisher, Four Courts Press' output includes books in the guides, archives, reference and history categories; it also sells the Maynooth research guides for local history. Some books of interest are:

- Clarke, Mary and Refausse, Raymond, *Directory of Historic Dublin Guilds*, 2nd edition, 2023
- Herlihy, Jim, *The Black & Tans, 1920–1921*, 2021
- Wallace, W.J.R., *The Vestry Records of the Parishes of St Bride, St Michael Le Pole and St Stephen, Dublin, 1662–1742*, 2011

Genealogical Publishing Company
https://genealogical.com
Based in Baltimore, Maryland, the Genealogical Publishing Company has an impressive number of Irish genealogical books on offer in a range of formats, many of which are reprints of older publications. A few of the titles for sale are:

- Adams, Raymond D., *An Alphabetical Index to Ulster Emigrants to Philadelphia*, 2006
- Clare, Rev. Wallace, *A Guide to Copies and Abstracts of Irish Wills*, 2008
- Mitchell, Brian, *A Guide to Irish Churches and Graveyards*, 2001

Geography Publications
www.geographypublications.com
Based in Dublin books for sale from Geography Publications include histories and biographies. Some of the titles are:

- Flood, John, *Kilcash and the Butlers of Ormond*, 2021
- O'Donnell, Michael, *Fethard, County Tipperary 1200–2000*, 2010
- A series of history and society books on individual counties such as Kerry, Westmeath, Leitrim and Roscommon

Irish Manuscripts Commission
www.irishmanuscripts.ie
The IMC publishes the *Analecta Hibernica* journal and also a range of books that contain primary sources for the history and culture of Ireland. One such recent book was *The Irish Religious Censuses of the 1760s: Catholics and Protestants in Eighteenth-Century Ireland*, by Brian Gurrin, Kerby A. Miller and Liam Kennedy.

Available for free download on its website are out of print editions such as:

- Keane, Edward et al., *King's Inns Admission Papers 1607–1867*, 1982
- Simington, Robert C., *The Civil Survey 1654–1656 Vol VII, County of Dublin*, 1945
- Simington, Robert C., *Books of Survey and Distribution, Vol II, County of Mayo*, 1956

North of Ireland Family History Society (NIFHS)
www.nifhs.org
Based in Newtownabbey, County Antrim, NIFHS publishes a number of guides and gravestone inscription books such as:

- NIFHS, *Researching Your Ancestors in the North of Ireland; Census Records*, 2017
- NIFHS, *Researching Your Ancestors in the North of Ireland: City of Belfast*, 2021
- Omagh Family History Society, *Tombstones of the Omey, County Tyrone*, 2nd edition, 2022

Pen & Sword Books
www.pen-and-sword.co.uk
Pen & Sword Books has a large number of history titles along with a good range of genealogy reference books. Some of the titles of interest are:

- Gibney, John, *The Irish Diaspora*, 2022
- Maxwell, Ian, *Tracing Your Irish Ancestors*, 2021
- Paton, Chris, *Tracing Your Irish Ancestors Through Land Records*, 2021

Society of Genealogists (SOG)
www.sog.org.uk
The SOG publishes a number of generic books in the My Ancestor was— series along with others that may include information to assist with Irish research. Some titles of interest are:

- Stewart, Alan, *My Ancestor was Irish*, 2nd edition, 2015
- Waller, Ian, *My Ancestor was in the Royal Navy*, 2014
- Webb, Cliff, *Dates and Calendars for the Genealogist*, 2015

Appendix

USEFUL ADDRESSES

Many of these organisations have online catalogues on their websites and some also have a range of resources that have been digitised and made freely available.

Before visiting any of these locations, you are advised to contact them beforehand to check opening times and availability of archival material.

You may also be expected to complete a registration as a researcher – further information is available on the relevant websites.

To search for specific items held in various archives, the Irish Archives Resource **www.iar.ie** is a free online database which contains searchable archival descriptions of collections throughout Ireland and Northern Ireland.

Another useful tool is RASCAL **www.rascal.ac.uk** which is an electronic gateway to research resources relating to Ireland. The site can be used to search or browse information about a wide range of research and special collections held in libraries, museums and archives in Ireland and abroad.

Armagh County Museum
The Mall East
Armagh
County Armagh
Northern Ireland
BT61 9BE
Telephone: +44 (0)28 3752 3070
Email: sarah.millsopp@armaghbanbridgecraigavon.gov.uk
Web: **www.visitarmagh.com**

Carlow County Archives and Central Library
Tullow Street
Carlow
County Carlow
Ireland
Telephone: +353 (0)59 912 9705
Email: library@carlowcoco.ie
Web: **www.carlowlibraries.ie**

Carlow County Museum and Carlow Tourist Office
College Street
Carlow Town
County Carlow
Ireland
R93 E3T2
Telephone: +353 (0)59 913 1554
Email: museum@carlowcoco.ie
Web: **www.carlowmuseum.com**

Cavan County Library and Local Studies
Johnson Central Library
Farnham Centre
Farnham Street
Cavan
County Cavan
Ireland
H12 V3W4
Telephone: +353 (0)49 437 8505
Email: library@cavancoco.ie
Web: **www.cavanlibrary.ie**

Cavan County Museum
Virginia Road
Ballyjamesduff
County Cavan
Ireland
A82 YP70
Telephone: +353 (0)49 854 4070
Email: info@cavanmuseum.ie
Web: **www.cavanmuseum.ie/home**

Clare County Archives
New Road
Ennis
County Clare
Ireland
V95 DXP2
Telephone: +353 (0)65 684 6414 or +353 (0)65 684 6269
Email: archivesrecords@clarecoco.ie
Web: **www.clarecoco.ie/services/library/clare-county-archives**

Clare County Library Local Studies Centre
Clare County Library
The Manse
Harmony Row
Ennis
County Clare
Ireland
V95 R236
Telephone: +353 (0)65 684 6271
Email: localstudies@clarelibrary.ie
Web: **www.clarelibrary.ie/eolas/library/local-studies/locstudi1.htm**

Cork City and County Archives
32 Great William O'Brien Street
Cork
County Cork
Ireland
T23 WP82
Telephone: +353 (0)21 450 5876
Email: archivist@corkcity.ie
Web: **www.corkarchives.ie**

Cork City Libraries
57–61 Grand Parade
Cork
County Cork
Ireland
T12 NT99
Telephone: +353 (0)21 492 4900
Email: libraries@corkcity.ie
Web: **www.corkcitylibraries.ie/en/**

Cork Public Museum
Fitzgerald Park
Mardyke Walk
Cork
County Cork
Ireland
Telephone: +353 (0)21 427 0679
Email: museum@corkcity.ie
Web: **www.corkcity.ie/en/cork-public-museum/museum-home**

Donegal Central Library Local Studies
Oliver Plunkett Road
Letterkenny
County Donegal
Ireland
F92 R273
Telephone: +353 (0)74 912 4950
Email: central@donegallibrary.ie
Web: **www.donegallibrary.ie/localfamilyhistory**

Donegal County Archives
Three Rivers Centre
Lifford
County Donegal
Ireland
F93 PN3H
Telephone: +353 (0)74 915 3900
Email: archivist@donegalcoco.ie
Web: **www.donegalcoco.ie/culture/archive**

Donegal County Museum
High Road
Letterkenny
County Donegal
Ireland
F92 K123
Telephone: +353 (0)74 912 4613
Email: museum@donegalcoco.ie
Web: **www.donegalcoco.ie/culture/countymuseum**

Down County Museum
The Mall
Downpatrick
County Down
Northern Ireland
BT30 6AH
Telephone: 0330 137 4049
Email: museums@nmandd.org
Web: www.newrymournedown.org/down-county-museum-downpatrick

Dublin Central Library
Ilac Shopping Centre
Henry Street
Dublin 1
Ireland
D01 DY80
Telephone: +353 (0)1 222 8300
Email: centrallibrary@dublincity.ie
Web: **www.dublincity.ie/residential/libraries/find-library/central-library**

Dublin City Library and Archive
139–144 Pearse Street
Dublin 2
Ireland
D02 HE37
Telephone: +353 (0)1 222 4999
Email: cityarchives@dublincity.ie
Web: **www.dublincity.ie/residential/libraries/find-library/dublin-city-library-and-archive**

Fermanagh County Museum
Enniskillen Castle
Enniskillen
County Fermanagh
Northern Ireland
BT74 7HL
Telephone: +44 (0)28 6632 5000
Email: castle@fermanaghomagh.com
Web: **www.enniskillencastle.co.uk**

Fingal Local Studies and Archives
46 Main Street
Swords
County Dublin
Ireland
Telephone: +353 (0)1 870 4496
Email: archives@fingal.ie
Web: **www.fingal.ie/council/service/archives**

Galway City Museum
Spanish Parade
Galway
County Galway
Ireland
H91 CX5P
Telephone: +353 (0)9 153 2460
Email: museum@galwaycity.ie
Web: **www.galwaycitymuseum.ie**

Galway County Council Archives
Galway County Libraries HQ
Island House
Cathedral Square
Galway
County Galway
Ireland
H91 RYC9
Telephone: +353 (0)91 509 388
Email: archivist@galwaycoco.ie
Web: **www.galway.ie/en/services/more/archives**

Genealogical Society of Ireland (GSI)
An Daonchartlann (archive)
Loughlinstown Drive
Dún Laoghaire
County Dublin
Ireland
Email: eolas@familyhistory.ie
Web: **www.familyhistory.ie**

Heritage Library – Cultural Heritage Service Library Armagh
Armagh Regional Administration Centre
1 Markethill Road
Armagh
County Armagh
Northern Ireland
BT60 1NR
Telephone: +44 (0)28 3752 7851
Email: armaghirishandlocal@librariesni.org.uk
Web: www.librariesni.org.uk/libraries

Heritage Library – Ballymena Central Library
5 Pat's Brae
Ballymena
County Antrim
Northern Ireland
BT43 5AX
Telephone: +44 (0)28 2563 3950
Email: ballymena.heritage@librariesni.org.uk
Web: www.librariesni.org.uk/libraries

Heritage Library – Belfast Central Library and the Newspaper Library
Royal Avenue
Belfast
County Antrim
Northern Ireland
BT1 1EA
Telephone: +44 (0)28 9050 9156
Email: belfast.heritage@librariesni.org
Web: www.librariesni.org.ukl/libraries

Heritage Library – Derry Central Library
35 Foyle Street
Derry
County Londonderry
Northern Ireland
BT48 6AL
Telephone: +44 (0)28 7122 9990
Email: derrycentral.library@librariesni.org.uk
Web: www.librariesni.org.uk/libraries

Heritage Library – Downpatrick Library
Market Street
Downpatrick
County Down
Northern Ireland
BT30 6LZ
Telephone: +44 (0)28 4433 3980 or +44 (0)28 4461 2895
Email: localstudies.down@librariesni.org.uk
Web: **www.librariesni.org.uk/libraries**

Heritage Library – Enniskillen Library
Hall's Lane
Enniskillen
County Fermanagh
Northern Ireland
BT74 7DR
Telephone: +44 (0)28 6632 2886
Email: enniskillen.library@librariesni.org.uk
Web: **www.librariesni.org.uk/libraries**

Heritage Library – Mellon Centre for Migration Studies
Ulster American Folk Park
2 Mellon Road
Omagh
County Tyrone
Northern Ireland
BT78 5QU
Telephone: +44 (0)28 8225 6315
Email: mcms@librariesni.org.uk
Website: **www.mellonmigrationcentre.com**

Heritage Library – Newry City Library
9 Hill Street
Newry
County Down
Northern Ireland
BT34 1DG
Telephone: +44 (0)28 3044 7423 or +44 (0)28 3026 4683
Email: newry.heritage@librariesni.org.uk
Web: **www.librariesni.org.uk/libraries**

Heritage Library – Omagh Library
Spillars Place
Omagh
County Tyrone
Northern Ireland
BT78 1HL
Telephone: +44 (0)28 8244 0733
Email: omagh.library@librariesni.org.uk
Web: **www.librariesni.org.uk/libraries**

Irish Family History Society
42 Mount Eagle Grove
Leopardstown Heights
Dublin
Ireland
D18 C8K3
Web: **https://ifhs.ie**

Irish Genealogical Research Society (IGRS) – UK and Rest of the World
18 Stratford Avenue
Rainham
Gillingham
Kent
England
ME8 0EP
Email: honsecretary@irishancestors.ie
Web: **www.irishancestors.ie**

Irish Genealogical Research Society (IGRS) – Irish Branch
10 Wellpark Avenue
Drumcondra
Dublin 9
Ireland
Email: ibhonsecretary@irishancestors.ie
Web: **www.irishancestors.ie**

Kerry County Museum
Ashe Memorial Hall
Denny Street
Tralee
County Kerry

Ireland
V92 CXE3
Telephone: +353 (0)66 712 7777
Email: info@kerrymuseum.ie
Web: **www.kerrymuseum.ie**

Kerry Library Local History and Archives
Tralee Library
Moyderwell
Tralee
County Kerry
Ireland
V92 X092
Telephone: +353 (0)66 712 1200
Email: localhistory@kerrylibrary.ie
Web: **www.kerrylibrary.ie/local-history-archives.html**

Kildare Library Local Studies, Genealogy and Archives
Riverbank Arts Centre
Main Street
Newbridge
County Kildare
Ireland
W12 D962
Telephone Local Studies: +353 (0)87 165 1888
Telephone Archives: +353 (0)87 693 8686
Email Local Studies: localhistory@kildarecoco.ie
Email Archives: archives@kildarecoco.ie
Web: **www.kildarecoco.ie/library/LocalStudiesGenealogyandArchives**

Kilkenny Archives Ltd
St. Kieran's College Campus
College Road
Kilkenny
County Kilkenny
Ireland
R95 Y99T
Telephone: +353 (0)85 243 1208
Email Archivist: kerevanjp@googlemail.com
Web: **www.kilkennyarchives.ie**

Kilkenny County Library and Local Studies
John's Green House
John's Green
Kilkenny
County Kilkenny
Ireland
R95 YH61
Telephone: +353 (0)56 779 4160
Email: info@kilkennylibrary.ie
Web: **www.kilkennylibrary.ie**

Laois County Library HQ
The Old Mill
Church Street
Portlaoise
County Laois
Ireland
R32 HDA3
Telephone: +353 (0)57 868 9338
Email: library@laoiscoco.ie
Web: **www.laoislibraries.ie**

Laois Local Studies and County Archives
Laois County Library Headquarters
The Old Mill
Church Street
Portlaoise
County Laois
Ireland
R32 HDA3
Telephone: +353 (0)57 868 9338
Email: localstudies@laoiscoco.ie
Web: **www.laoislocalstudies.ie**

Leitrim County Library and Local Studies
Main Street
Ballinamore
County Leitrim
Ireland
Telephone Library: +353 (0)71 964 5582
Telephone Local Studies: +353 (0)71 964 5567

Email Library: leitrimlibrary@leitrimcoco.ie
Email Local Studies: localstudies@leitrimcoco.ie
Web: **www.leitrimcoco.ie/eng/community-culture/library**

Libraries Ireland
www.librariesireland.ie

Libraries Northern Ireland
www.librariesni.org.uk

Limerick Archives
Merchant's Quay
Limerick
County Limerick
Ireland
Telephone: +353 (0)61 557 293
Email: archives@limerick.ie
Web: **www.limerick.ie/archives**

Limerick City Library
Barrow House
Michael Street
Limerick
County Limerick
Ireland
V94 RF63
Telephone: +353 (0)61 557 510
Email: citylibrary@limerick.ie
Web: **www.limerick.ie/council/services/community-and-leisure/libraries**

Limerick Local Studies
Watch House Cross Community Library
Moyross
Limerick
County Limerick
Ireland
Telephone: +353 (0)61 557 726
Email: localstudies@limerick.ie
Web: **www.localstudies.limerick.ie/Library/LocalStudies**

Limerick Museum
The Old Franciscan Friary
Henry Street
Limerick
County Limerick
Telephone: +353 (0)61 557 740
Email: museum@limerick.ie
Web: **www.limerick.ie/limerick-museum**

Linen Hall Library
17 Donegall Square North
Belfast
County Antrim
Northern Ireland
BT1 5GB
Telephone: +44 (0)28 9032 1707
Email: info@linenhall.com
Web: **www.linenhall.com**

Longford County Library, Archives and Local Studies
Longford Branch Library
Longford
County Longford
Ireland
Phone: +353 (0)43 334 0727
Email: library@longfordcoco.ie
Web: **www.longfordlibrary.ie**

Louth County Archives
Old Gaol
Ardee Road
Dundalk
County Louth
Ireland
A91 PY17
Telephone: +353 (0)42 932 4358
Email: archive@louthcoco.ie
Web: **www.louthcoco.ie/en/services/archives**

Louth County Library and Local Studies
Dundalk Library
Roden Place
Dundalk
County Louth
Ireland
A91 RC44
Telephone: +353 (0)42 935 3190
Email: libraryhelpdesk@louthcoco.ie
Web: **www.louthcoco.ie/en/services/library**

Louth County Museum
Carroll Centre
Roden Place
Jocelyn Street
Dundalk
County Louth
Ireland
Telephone: +353 (0)42 939 2999
Email: museum@louthcoco.ie
Web: **www.louthcoco.ie/en/services/county-museum**

Marsh's Library
St Patrick's Close
Dublin
Ireland
D08 FK79
Telephone: +353 (0)1 454 3511
Email: information@marshlibrary.ie
Web: **www.marshlibrary.ie**

Mayo County Library Local History Department
John Moore Road
Castlebar
County Mayo
Ireland
Telephone: +353 (0)94 904 7953
Email: mcostell@mayococo.ie
Web: **www.mayo.ie/library/local-history**

Meath County Library Local Studies
Railway Street
Navan
County Meath
Ireland
C15 RW31
Telephone: +353 (0)46 902 1134
Email: navanlib@meathcoco.ie
Web: **www.meath.ie/council/council-services/libraries/local-studies-and-family-history**

Monaghan County Library Local Studies
98 Avenue
Clones
County Monaghan
Ireland
H23 RW70
Telephone: +353 (0)47 74712 or +353 (0)47 74713
Email Library: cloneslibrary@monaghancoco.ie
Email Local Studies: clennon@monaghancoco.ie
Web: **www.monaghan.ie/library/local-history**

Monaghan County Museum
1–2 Hill Street
Monaghan
County Monaghan
Ireland
Telephone: +353 (0)47 82928
Email: comuseum@monaghancoco.ie
Web: **www.monaghan.ie/museum**

National Archives of Ireland (NAI)
Bishop Street
Dublin 8
Ireland
D08 DF85
Telephone: +353 (0)1 407 2300
Email: query@nationalarchives.ie
Web: **www.nationalarchives.ie**

National Library of Ireland (NLI)
7–8 Kildare Street
Dublin 2
Ireland
D02 P638
Telephone: +353 (0)1 603 0200
Email: info@nli.ie
Web: **www.nli.ie/en/homepage.aspx**

North of Ireland Family History Society (NIFHS) Research Centre
Unit C4 Valley Business Centre
67 Church Road
Newtownabbey
County Antrim
Northern Ireland
BT36 7LS
Email: bookings@nifhs.org
Web: **www.nifhs.org**

Offaly County Library Local Studies
Tullamore Library
Bridge Lane
Tullamore
County Offaly
Ireland
Telephone: +353 (0)57 934 6832
Email: tullamorelibrary@offalycoco.ie
Web: **www.offaly.ie/eng/Services/Libraries/Local-Studies/Local-Studies**

Offaly Archives
Unit 1F, Axis Business Park
Clara Road
Tullamore
County Offaly
Ireland
Email: archivist@offalyhistory.com or info@offalyhistory.com
Web: **www.offalyarchives.com**

Oireachtas Library and Research Service
Leinster House
Kildare Street

Dublin 2
Ireland
D02 XR20
Telephone: +353 (0)1 618 4701
Email: library.and.research@oireachtas.ie
Web: **www.oireachtas.ie/en/how-parliament-is-run/houses-of-the-oireachtas-service/library-and-research-service/**

Public Records Office Northern Ireland (PRONI)
2 Titanic Boulevard
Belfast
County Antrim
Northern Ireland
BT3 9HQ
Telephone: +44 (0)28 9053 4800
Email: proni@communities-ni.gov.uk
Web: **www.nidirect.gov.uk/campaigns/public-record-office-northern-ireland-proni**

Roscommon County Library Archives and Local Studies
Abbey Street
Roscommon
County Roscommon
Ireland
F42 RP49
Telephone Roscommon Branch Library: +353 (0)90 663 7277
Telephone Local Studies: +353 (0)90 663 7273
Email: library@roscommoncoco.ie
Web: **www.roscommoncoco.ie/en/services/community/library/local_studies_and_archives**

Royal Irish Academy
19 Dawson Street
Dublin 2
Ireland
D02 HH58
Telephone: +353 (0)1 609 0600
Email: info@ria.ie
Web: **www.ria.ie/library**

Sligo County Library Local Studies and Archive
Bridge Street
Sligo
County Sligo
Ireland
F91 PTX8
Telephone: +353 (0)71 911 1674
Email: sligolib@sligococo.ie
Web: **www.sligolibrary.ie/local-studies-and-reference**

Sligo County Museum
Stephen Street
Sligo
County Sligo
Ireland
F91 X264
Telephone: +353 (0)71 911 1679
Email: sligomuseum@sligococo.ie
Web: **www.sligolibrary.ie/museum**

Society of Genealogists (SOG)
2/40 Wharf Road,
London
N1 7GS
Tel: +44 (0)20 7251 8799
Email: librarian@sog.org.uk
Web: **www.sog.org.uk**

Tipperary County Library – Tipperary Studies
The Source Library and Arts Centre
Thurles Branch Library
Cathedral Street
Thurles
County Tipperary
Ireland
Telephone: +353 (0)52 616 6123
Email: studies@tipperarycoco.ie
Web: **www.tipperarystudies.ie**

Tipperary Museum of Hidden History
Mick Delahunty Square
Clonmel
County Tipperary
Ireland
E91 Y891
Telephone: +353 (0)52 616 5252
Email: museum@tipperarycoco.ie
Web: **www.hiddenhistory.ie**

Ulster Historical Foundation (UHF)
Bradley Thallon House,
Unit 44D, Kiltonga Estate
Belfast Road
Newtownards
County Down
Northern Ireland
BT23 4TJ
Telephone: +44 (0)28 91 812 073
Email: enquiry@uhf.org.uk
Web: **www.ancestryireland.com**

Ulster Museum
Stranmillis Road
Botanic Gardens
Belfast
Northern Ireland
BT9 5AB
Telephone: +44 (0)28 9044 0000
Email: info@nationalmuseumsni.org
Web: **www.ulstermuseum.org**

Waterford City Archives
High Street
Waterford
County Waterford
Ireland
Telephone: +353 (0)58 21 144
Email: archivist@waterfordcouncil.ie
Web:**www.waterfordcouncil.ie/departments/culture-heritage/archives/index.htm**

Waterford County Archive
Dungarven Library
Davitt's Quay
Dungarvan
County Waterford
Ireland
Telephone: +353 (0)58 21 144
Email: archivist@waterfordcouncil.ie
Web: **www.waterfordcouncil.ie/departments/culture-heritage/archives/ index.htm**

Waterford City Central Library Local Studies
Lady Lane
Waterford
County Waterford
Ireland
Telephone: +353 (0)51 849 975
Email: lstudies@waterfordcouncil.ie
Web: **www.waterfordlibraries.ie/local-studies**

Waterford County Museum
St Augustine Street
Dungarvan
County Waterford
Ireland
Telephone: +353 (0)58 45 960
Email: history@waterfordmuseum.ie
Web: **www.waterfordmuseum.ie**

Westmeath County Archives Department
Westmeath County Library Headquarters
County Buildings
Mount Street
Mullingar
County Westmeath
Ireland
Telephone: +353 (0)44 933 2162
Email: library@westmeathcoco.ie
Web: **www.westmeathcoco.ie/en/ourservices/library/explorewestmeath/ localstudies/archives**

Westmeath Libraries
Mullingar Library Local Studies
County Buildings
Mount Street
Mullingar
Westmeath
Ireland
N91 XH9R
Telephone: +353 (0)44 933 2161
Email: mgarlib@westmeathcoco.ie
Web: **www.westmeathcoco.ie/en/ourservices/library/explorewestmeath/ localstudies**

Westmeath County Local Studies
Aidan Heavy Library
Athlone Civic Centre
Church Street
Athlone
County Westmeath
Ireland
N37 N625
Telephone: +353 (0)90 644 2157
Email: athlib@westmeathcoco.ie
Web: **www.westmeathcoco.ie/en/ourservices/library/explorewestmeath/ localstudies**

Wexford County Archive
6A Ardcavan Business Park
Ardcavan
County Wexford
Ireland
Telephone: +353 (0)53 919 6572
Email: archivist@wexfordcoco.ie
Web: **www.wexfordcountyarchive.com**

Wexford Library Local Studies (Main Collection)
Library Headquarters
County Hall
Carricklawn
County Wexford
Y35 WY93

Telephone: +353 (0)53 919 6561
Email: wexfordlib@wexfordcoco.ie.
Web: **www.wexfordcoco.ie/libraries/more-library-services/local-studies-service**

Wexford Library Local Studies (Microfilm Collection)
Wexford Library
Mallin Street
Wexford
County Wexford
Ireland
Y35 AY20
Telephone: +353 (0)53 919 6760
Email: wexfordlibrary@wexfordcoco.ie
Web: **www.wexfordcoco.ie/libraries/more-library-services/local-studies-service**

Wicklow Library and Archives
The Mall
Wicklow Town
County Wicklow
Ireland
A67 X504
Telephone: +353 (0)40 420 100
Email: archives@wicklowcoco.ie
Web: **www.wicklow.ie/Living/Services/Arts-Heritage-Archives/Archives/Our-Service**

Wicklow County Library Local Studies
Salthouse Lane
Wicklow Town
County Wicklow
Ireland
A67 X504
Telephone: +353 (0)87 268 3724
Email: wicklowlocalstudies@wicklowcoco.ie
Web: **www.wicklow.ie/Living/Services/Libraries/Local-Studies**

BIBLIOGRAPHY AND SOURCES

Adams, J.R.R., *Merchants in Plenty: Joseph Symth's Belfast Directories of 1807 and 1808,* (Ulster Historical Foundation, Belfast, 1991)

Andrews, Helen. 2009. 'Burke, John'. In: *Dictionary of Irish Biography.* **www.dib.ie**

Connolly, S.J., *The Oxford Companion to Irish History,* (Oxford University Press, Oxford, 1998)

Day, Angelique and McWilliams, Patrick, (eds). *Parishes of Co Londonderry 1, 1830, 1834, 1836. Ordnance Survey Memoirs of Ireland, Vol 6,* (Institute of Irish Studies, Belfast, 1990)

Grenham, John, *Tracing Your Irish Ancestors,* 5th edition, (Gill Books, Dublin, 2019)

Helferty, S. and Refaussé, R., *Directory of Irish Archives,* 5th edition, (Four Courts Press, Dublin, 2011)

Herber, Mark, *Ancestral Trails,* (Sutton Publishing, Gloucestershire, 2007)

Lysaght, Charles. 2009. 'MacLysaght, Edward Anthony Edgeworth'. In: *Dictionary of Irish Biography.* **www.dib.ie**

McWilliams, Patrick, *Ordnance Survey Memoirs of Ireland, Index of People and Places.* (Institute of Irish Studies, Belfast, 2002)

Maxwell, Ian, *Tracing Your Northern Irish Ancestors,* (Pen & Sword Books, Barnsley, 2013)

Paton, Chris, *Tracing Your Irish Family History on the Internet,* (Pen & Sword Books, Barnsley, 2019)

Roulston, William J., *Researching Ulster Ancestors,* (Ulster Historical Foundation, Belfast, 2018)

Woods, C.J., 1980. 'A Guide to Irish Biographical Dictionaries'. *The Maynooth Review.* Vol. 6, No 1 (May), pp.16–34. **www.jstor.org/stable/20556942**

INDEX

Act of Union 1800, 25, 27, 70
Allen County Public Library, Fort Wayne, 12, 39–40, 83
Ancestry, 8, 15–17, 22, 47, 55, 58, 60, 67, 68, 75, 88
Ancestry, card catalogue, 16
Ancestry, newspapers by, 15–16
Armagh County Museum, 94
Armagh Cultural Heritage Service Library, County Armagh, 100
Artrea Parish, County Londonderry, 77
Ask About Ireland, 68, 86
Asquith, Mr, 25
Aylmer, Elinor, 27

Ballymena, County Antrim, x, xx, 11, 21, 77, 100
Ballymena, Central Library, 5, 100
Ballymena, Church Street, xxi, xxiii
Ballymena, Galgorm Street, xix
Ballymena, Mill Street, xix
Ballymena, Wellington Street, xx
Ballymoney, County Antrim, 90
Bangor, County Down, 25
Barony of Armagh, County Armagh, voters, 25
Barony of Tiranny, County Armagh, voters, 25
Benn, George, 82
Black, George Fraser, 83
Blackstaff Press, 91

Blackwood, Sir James, 7, 28
Books Ireland, 35, 78, 91
Boyle, James, 77
Bradshaw, Hugh William, xiii–xvii
Bradshaw, John, xiv
Bradshaw, William, xiv
British Newspaper Archive (The) (BNA), xix, 11, 13–14
BNA, free access, 14
Bourke, General, 29
Bourne, Edward Esq., 29
Burke, John, 46
Burke, Sir John Bernard, 46
Burke's Peerage, 47
Burtchaell, George, 20
Butler, Theobald Fitz-Walter, Lord Dunboyne, 20
Byrne family, County Wicklow, 75

Canada, 15, 18, 24, 27
Cappawhite, County Tipperary, xiv, xv
Carlisle, Nicholas, 71–3
Carlow Castle, 70
Carlow County Archives and Central Library, 95
Carlow County Museum and Carlow Tourist Office, 95
Carrickfergus Assize, County Antrim, 82
Carrol, Catherine, 29
Carrol, General Sir William P., 29
Carrol, William, 29

Carnmore, County Galway, xxiv, xxvi
Casey, Albert, 88
Castleblaney, County Monaghan, 26
Castlegar, County Galway, xxii, xxv
Cavan County Library and Local Studies, 95
Cavan County Museum, 95
Church of Ireland histories, 88
CIGO, xii, 35
Civic Access Borrower Scheme, 6
Clanchy, Captain Henry, 26
Clare County Archives, 96
Clare County Library and Local Studies Centre, 20, 96
Clarke, Peter J. Blogspot, 55
Cliftonville Presbyterian Church, Belfast, xix
Cokayne, George Edward, 47
Colby, Colonel Thomas, 76
Coleraine, County Londonderry, 23
Collins, Michael, 45
Comber, County Down, 28
Congregation of Sisters of Mercy, 89
Connolly, Eddie, 28
Connor, Roger, 43
Conway, Mr, xiv
Connaught, 38
Coote, Sir Charles, 75
Cork City and County Archives, 45, 63, 96
Cork City Library, 59, 96
Cork Past and Present, 45
Cork Public Museum, 97
Cosgrove, William, 45
County Cork, xv, 14, 29, 31, 42–3, 45, 53, 59, 62–3, 65, 79, 86, 88
County Galway, xxiv, xxv, xxvi, 66, 86–7
County Kerry, xvi, 60, 62–3, 88, 92
County Kildare, 84
County Laois, 26
County Leitrim, 28, 78, 92
County Longford, 12, 28
County Mayo, xxv, 30, 93
County Meath, 14, 76
County Offaly, 61, 84
County Roscommon, 28, 92

County Westmeath, 28, 92
County Wicklow, 70, 72–4, 75, 88
Cousley, Annie, xxiii
Culfeightrin Parish, County Antrim, 90
Cullybackey, xix–xx

de Montfort, Simon, 28
De Valera, Éamon, 45
Derry Central Library, County Londonderry, 5, 100
Derrykeighan Parish, County Antrim, 90
DIB, xii, 45–6, 69
DNB, xii, 43–4
Dobson, David, 88
Donegal Central Library Local Studies, 97
Donegal County Archives, 97
Donegal County Museum, 97
Down County Museum, 98
Downpatrick Library, County Down, 5, 101, 121
Drogheda, 10, 12, 14, 56, 65–6
Dublin, Central Library, 98
Dublin, City Library and Archives, 8, 56, 58, 89, 98
Dublin Exchange, 25
Dublin, Hospital and Free Scholl of King Charles II, 34
Dublin, Marsh's Library, 8, 107
Dublin, PRO, 26, 51
Dublin, Royal Charter School Clontarf, 38
Dublin, University College, 68
Duke of Wellington, 76
Dun Laoghaire, County Dublin, 24, 99

Earl of Cork, Richard, 1st Earl, 42–3
Enniskillen Library, County Fermanagh, 5, 101

Fagan, Helen, 27
Fagan, Richard, 27
Fáilte Romhat, 58
Family Search, 48, 55, 63, 83–4
Fanning, Aengus, 46

Farrar, Henry, 31
Fermanagh County Museum, 98
Ffolliott, Rosemary, 30
Findmypast, 13–14, 16, 30, 33, 45, 47, 50–1, 55–8, 60, 63–5, 67–8, 88
Findmypast, free access, 14
Fingal Local Studies and Archives, 90, 99
First World War, 49–50, 89
Fitz-Aldelm, William, 74
Fitzgerald, Maurice, 74
Fitzgerald, Walter, 84
Fitzwilliam, William, 75
Flatman, Frances Annie, xix
Flatman, George, xix
Flatman, Maud, xx
FLHS, 35
Flyleaf Press, 92
Four Courts Press, 92
Free Irish E-books Index, 85
FULS, xii

Galway City Museum, 99
Galway County Council Archives, 99
Gazette, Church of Ireland, 15
Genealogy Gophers, 84
Genealogical Publishing Company, 92
Geography Publications, 92
Google Books, 23, 41, 44, 47, 55, 57–8, 63–5, 67–8, 73, 75–6, 79, 82, 86
Google News, 18
Gordon family of County Antrim, xix–xxiii
Gray, Doctor John, 26
Grealish / Greelish, James, xxiv
Grealish / Greelish, Peter, xxiv, xxv, xxvi
Grealish, Winifred, xxiv
Great Famine, xxvii, xxviii, xxix
GSI, xxii, 33, 99

Hamlin, Mr, 56
Hansbrow, Reverend George, 70, 72–3
Harper, Arthur, 26

Harper, John, 26
Hathi Trust, 47, 55, 57, 67–8, 70, 83, 86
Heritage Library – Ballymena Central Library, 5, 100
Heritage Library – Belfast Central Library and the Newspaper Library, 4–5, 100
Heritage Library – Cultural Heritage Service Library Armagh, 6, 100
Heritage Library – Derry Central Library, 5, 100
Heritage Library – Downpatrick Library, 5, 101
Heritage Library – Enniskillen Library, 5, 101
Heritage Library – Mellon Centre for Migration Studies, 5, 101
Heritage Library – Newry City Library, 6, 101
Heritage Library – Omagh Library, 6, 102
Hillman family of Aughrim, County Londonderry, 78
Holmes, Reverend Dean, Vicar of Kilmore, 29
Hurley, John, xvi
Hurley, Maria Theresa, xvi–xvii
Hurley, Mr, xiv, xvi

IFHS, xii, 34, 102
IGRS, xii, 26–7, 34, 59, 102
IHO, xii, 37
IMC, xii, 48, 93
Institute of Irish Studies, 21, 77
Internet Archive, xxv, 39, 42–5, 47–8, 55–7, 65, 67–8, 72–3, 75, 79–80, 82, 86
Iris Oifigiúil, 52
Irish Bulletin, 51
Irish Capuchin Provincial Archives, 90
Irish Ecclesiastical Gazette, 15
Irish Family History Centre, 36
Irish Newspaper Archive, 8, 11–12, 16
Irish Times Archive, 15

Jacobites, 89
Joseph McGarrity Newspaper Collection, 18
Joy, Henry, 82
JSTOR, 35, 37–9

Kerry County Museum, 102
Kerry Library Local History and Archives, 103
Kildare Library Local Studies, Genealogy and Archives, 103
Kilkenny Archives Ltd, 103
Kilkenny County Library and Local Studies, 104
King's County (now County Offaly), 19, 61
Kirkinriola Parish, County Antrim, 77

Lagan, Elise ny, 82
Lally clan, 88
Laois County Library HQ, 104
Laois Local Studies and County Archives, 104
Leitrim County Library and Local Studies, 104
Lennon Wylie, 60
Lewis, Samuel, 74, 76
Libraries Ireland, 5, 20, 40, 86, 105
Libraries NI, 5–6, 20, 40, 86, 105
Limerick Archives, 105
Limerick City Library, 105
Limerick Local Studies, 105
Limerick Museum, 106
Linen Hall Library, 6–7, 21–2, 106
Longfield, Anne, 43
Longford County Library, Archives and Local Studies, 106
Lord Londonderry, 28
Louth County Archives, 106
Louth County Library and Local Studies, 107
Louth County Museum, 107
Lower Creggan, County Armagh, 25

McDonnell, Frances, 89
MacLysaght, Edward, 48

Marsh's Library, 8–9, 107
Mayo County Library Local History Department, 107
Meath County Library Local Studies, 108
Mockler, Richard, xiv
Monaghan County Library Local Studies, 108
Monaghan County Museum, 108
Montgomery, Mr, 56
Morissey, Doctor, xiii
Moyle, County Antrim, 90
Muskerry Yeomanry, 43
Mylod family of counties Offaly and Kildare, 84
My Heritage, 47, 55, 63, 65, 75, 89

Naillor, Elizabeth, 19
NEGHS, xii, 29
Neile, Thomas, 19
Nenagh, County Tipperary, 29
New York, USA, 2, 29–30, 78
New Zealand, 15, 24
Newsplan Project, 1–2, 11
Newtownabbey, County Antrim, 23, 35, 93, 109
Newtownards, County Down, 25, 112
Newry City Library, County Down, 6, 101
NLI, xii, 2–4, 20, 54, 109
NLI, Newsplan Report, 1–2
NLI, Sources database, 36
NIFHS, xii, 23, 34–5, 39, 93, 109
North America, 22
Northern Ireland Community Archive, 90

O'Connell, Daniel, 27
O'Donoghue, D.J., 44
O'Gribben, Brian, 82
O'Hart, John, 47–8, 88
O'Mullally clan, 88
O'Toole, Adam Duff, 43
O'Toole, Luke, 75
Offaly Archives, 109
Offaly County Library Local Studies, 109

Oireachtas Library and Research Service, 109
Omagh, County Tyrone, 6, 23, 93
Open Library, 47–8, 81, 86
Owens, Mr, 56

Palmer family of Rahan, County Kildare, 84
Parks, Constable Ross, xiv
Pen & Sword Books, 93
Pennefather, Mr, xv–xvi
Pennefather v. Hurley, xv
Pennsylvania University, 44
PERSI, 39–40
Philipstown, xiii, xivx, xvii
Philipstown House, xiv–xv
PHSI, xii, 23
Pike, W.T., 44–5
Poor Law Unions, xxvii, 66, 78
Potato blight, 78
Power family of Curraghmore, County Waterford, 34
Project Gutenberg, 84
PRONI, xii, 9–10, 110

Quakers, see Society of Friends
Queen's University, Belfast, 21, 77

Reddan, Nick, 28
Registry of Deeds, 26
RIA, xii, 37, 45, 56, 77, 110
Roscommon County Library Archives and Local Studies, 110
Royal Dublin Fusiliers Archive, 89
Ryan, Doctor John, xiv
Ryan, Richard, 41

Schlegel, Donald M., 22
Scully family, Rock of Cashel, 34
Seward, William Wenman, 69–70
Short, Mr Vere Dawson, xvi
Sligo County Library Local Studies and Archive, 111
Sligo County Museum, 111
Smythe-Wood, Doctor Patrick, 27
Society of Friends, 31, 73
SOG, xii, 26, 56, 93, 111
Strongbow, 74

Taylor, John, 27
Templemore Parish, County Londonderry, 77
Terry family, Spanish of Irish origin, 34
The Gazette, xxi, 20, 49–52
Thom, Alexander Thom and Co, 45, 59, 66–8
Tichborne, Sir Henry, Lord Ferrard, 56
Timeline Project, 29
Tipperary County Library – Tipperary Studies, 111
Tipperary Museum of Hidden History, 112
Toole, William, 82

UHF, xii, 25, 35, 59–60, 77, 112
Ulster History Circle, 46
United Irishmen, xvii, 4, 7, 43, 70, 89
Ulster Museum, 112
United States of America, 15, 18, 21
University of Louisiana, Lafayette, 21

Vicars, Sir Arthur, 31
Villanova University, Pennsylvania, 18

Warren, Judge, xv
Waterford City Archives, 112
Waterford County Archive, 113
Waterford County Museum, 113
Webb, Alfred, 43
Webb, Doctor Robert A., xiv
Weldon, Alicia, xv–xvi
Westmeath County Archives Department, 113
Westmeath Libraries, 114
Westmeath County Local Studies, 114
Wexford County Archive, 114
Wexford Library Local Studies (Main Collection), 114
Wexford Library Local Studies (Microfilm Collection), 115
Whiteboys, 43
Wicklow Library and Archives, 115

Wicklow County Library Local Studies, 115
Wicklow Town, County Wicklow, 70, 72–5
Wikisource, 44–5
Wills, Freeman, 42
Wills, James, 41–2

Wilson, Shane – Directory database, 55
Woodvale Road, Belfast, xxii
WorldCat, 39–41, 44–5, 47–8, 54, 69

Young, Robert M., 81–2